# MARX, PROUDHON

## and

# European Socialism

### is one of the volumes
### in the

## TEACH YOURSELF HISTORY
## LIBRARY

*Edited by* A. L. ROWSE

# Teach Yourself History

VOLUMES READY OR IN PREPARATION

# MARX, PROUDHON

## and

# European Socialism

by

J. HAMPDEN JACKSON

NEW YORK
THE MACMILLAN COMPANY

8934

PRINTED IN GREAT BRITAIN

# Contents

# A General Introduction
# to the Series

THIS series has been undertaken in the conviction that there can be no subject of study more important than history. Great as have been the conquests of natural science in our time—such that many think of ours as a scientific age *par excellence*—it is even more urgent and necessary that advances should be made in the social sciences, if we are to gain control of the forces of nature loosed upon us. The bed out of which all the social sciences spring is history; there they find, in greater or lesser degree, subject-matter and material verification or contradiction.

There is no end to what we can learn from history, if only we will, for it is coterminous with life. Its special field is the life of man in society, and at every point we can learn vicariously from the experience of others before us in history.

To make one point only—the understanding of politics : how can we hope to understand the world of affairs around us if we do not know how it came to be what it is ? How to understand Germany, or Soviet Russia or the United States—or ourselves, without knowing something of their history ?

There is no subject that is more useful, or indeed indispensable.

Some evidence of the growing awareness of this may be seen in the immense increase in the interest of the reading public in history, and the much larger place the subject has come to take in education in our time.

This series has been planned to meet the needs and demands of a very wide public and of education— they are indeed the same. I am convinced that the most congenial, as well as the most concrete and practical, approach to history is the biographical, through the lives of the great men whose actions have been so much part of history, and whose careers in turn have been so moulded and formed by events.

The key idea of this series, and what distinguishes it from any other that has appeared, is the intention by way of a biography of a great man to open up a significant historical theme; for example, Cromwell and the Puritan Revolution, or Lenin and the Russian Revolution.

My hope is, in the end, as the series fills out and completes itself, by a sufficient number of biographies to cover whole periods and subjects in that way. To give you the history of the United States, for example, or the British Empire or France, *via* a number of biographies of their leading historical figures.

That should be something new, as well as convenient and practical, in education.

I need hardly say that I am a strong believer in people with good academic standards writing once more for the general reading public, and of the public being given the best that the universities can provide. From this point of view this series is intended to bring the University into the homes of the people.

A. L. ROWSE.

ALL SOULS COLLEGE,
OXFORD.

*Chapter One*

# Prologue

THERE are two currents in the movement known as Socialism, and no story of the rise of that movement is worth reading unless it takes account of each. Looked at from the point of view of the mid-twentieth century, it may well seem that socialism has been moving always in the same direction, always towards the centralization of power and the increasing authority of the State. Not for nothing were the early Marxists called Authoritarians; not for nothing did Sidney and Beatrice Webb at the end of their lives find their Mecca in Moscow. All schools of Social Democracy from the Germans to the Fabians have preached centralization, and all schools of Communist Socialists from the Russians to the Yugoslavs and the Chinese have practised totalitarianism. Looking at the world today, socialists may well wonder if their creed offers any alternative to the course towards the omnicompetent State.

If they look back at the history of their own movement, they will find one. They will find a tradition known variously as libertarianism, individualism, mutualism, federalism, syndicalism : a tradition usually described as anarchism, which fought its first battle with the Marxists for the soul of socialism a century ago, and its latest, but surely not its last, in 1936, behind the lines of Republican Spain. They will find that the anarchist (no-ruler) tradition was stronger than that of Marx in the First Workers' International, which Marx disbanded—or removed to New York, it comes to the same thing—because so many of the workers' delegates were anarchists. They will find that their famous Paris Commune was the creation of men who called themselves mutualists or federalists, and were for the most part no followers of Marx. They will find that the most radical section of the French working-class movement was composed of syndicalists who opposed both the Marxist and the parliamentary branch of socialism. They will find that the revolutionary socialists who bore the heat and burden of the day in Switzerland, Italy and Spain were anarchists. And they may even find that the mass of the people in Russia in 1917 cast their votes against the Bolsheviks and for the Social Revolutionaries who stood nearer to the anarchist camp.

The father of this anarchist tradition was Proudhon, who died in 1865 when Marx had still eighteen years to live. It was Proudhon's errant disciple, Bakunin, who led the majority in the First International; Proudhon's apostles—Beslay, Courbet and Gambon among them—who led the Paris Communards; Proudhon's follower Sorel whose teaching was responsible for the charter which the French trade-union movement adopted at Amiens in 1906. It was Proudhon's writing which sowed the seed of anarchist socialism in Catalonia, and Proudhon's ideas, transmitted less directly, that took root among the social revolutionaries in Russia.

In the doctrinal hey-day of the mid-nineteenth century there was a great intellectual battle between the authoritarians and the anarchists, a battle eventually won by the former, with the result that the history of socialism, at least in continental Europe, has come to seem the history of various schools of Marxism. But if Karl Marx stands out today as the begetter of socialism, he is not the only begetter. Not only is there an anarchist, mutualist, anti-State tradition which is the opposite of Marxism, but there is also in the essence of the socialist creed a moral doctrine with which Marx, who professed a hearty contempt for moral preaching, had nothing to do. Socialism is an ethos as well as a policy, an attitude towards social life and an interpretation of one's duty towards one's neighbour, as well as a body of economic and political doctrine. And of this ethos Proudhon, though not the originator, was the major prophet.

To trace the origins of socialism would take us a long way back, but perhaps there is no need to look farther than the 1820s. The word "socialism" was not in use much before 1832 when a Frenchman, Pierre Leroux, defined it as "the exaggerated expression of the idea of association or of society," and the first time it appeared in print was probably November 1827, when Robert Owen, writing in his *Co-operative Magazine*, said that in the argument whether it is more beneficial that capital should be individual or common there are socialists or communists who held that it should be common. (The words "socialism" and "communism" were practically interchangeable until the time of Lenin.) If one had to fix a birthday for socialism, it would be somewhere in 1821 or 1822, years which saw the appearance of three books written by men who later were recognized as its forerunners.

The first was Robert Owen's *Report to the County of Lanark*. It was a full-blooded attack on the competitive system, and a forceful expression of an idea which was to be taken up by Proudhon and Marx in the next generation. This idea was that the value of a thing depends on the amount of labour incorporated in it, and that labour rather than money should measure the different values of commodities. Yet it was not as the proponent of the Labour Theory of Value, of which in any case he was not the originator, that Owen was to be known abroad, but as the founder of co-operative communities as a new model of social organization which, he fondly believed, the outside world would soon accept.

The second was Fourier's *Traité d'Association*. Like Owen, Fourier saw the evils of the capitalist system and, like Owen, he sought the solution in a new form of association which would begin with a Utopian village-community. Fourier envisaged his *phalanstères* as communal settlements of perhaps 1,600 men, women and children on 5,000 acres of land, each working according to his talents and tastes for the good of all. No benefactors came forward to found *phalanstères* in France, but after Fourier's death a few came forward in the United States and, oddly enough, in Russia and Spain. Fourier's main posthumous influence was through his general teaching on the value of communal activity for production and for social life.

The third was Saint-Simon's *Le Système industriel*. The Comte de Saint-Simon (1770–1825) was an older man than Owen or Fourier, and unlike them he had never had any contact with the working-class. He belonged to the aristocracy of the Ancien Régime, but he saw that the social rôle of the old ruling families was finished and that the future lay with the captains of industry. He called on the industrial classes, employers and workers, to adopt methods of scientifically organized production. He foresaw no conflict between them when he insisted that society must be organized for the welfare of the poor. In the 1850s his followers—especially Enfantin, Bazard and Pierre Leroux—made a great stir by their denunciation of inherited and unmerited wealth, and by their advocacy of what a century later would be called a planned economy.

The birthplace of socialism was not Britain, where it might have been expected—Britain where the industrial revolution had taken place first and most disconcertingly; Britain where the factory was replacing the workshop and the wage-earner the master-craftsman; Britain where there was already a proletariat and where the laws against workers organizing in trade unions were relaxed as early as 1822. The birthplace of socialism was France, where there was no industrial revolution worth the name, only a slow transformation lasting over a century. In the generation after the fall of Napoleon, France had still no proletariat in the sense of a numerous body of factory employees. The immense majority of French workers were on the land, and worked as owner-farmers rather than as landless labourers. The industrial working-class got their living in small workshops; they were craftsmen rather than members of a proletariat. If they organized at all, they organized illegally, for the Penal Code made striking and picketing a criminal offence and prohibited associations of more than twenty persons. In 1834 associations even of twenty persons were forbidden if they were part of a larger whole.

Compared with Britain, France seemed an un-
likely seedbed for socialism. Yet compared with any
continental country, except perhaps Belgium, France
had an urban civilization. The large towns, the
natural forcing-houses of socialism, were growing
fast. In 1801 about one in every fifteen of the population lived in towns of 20,000 or more people; in
1851 the proportion was rather more than one in
ten. In that period the population of Paris doubled,
rising from half a million to a million. This was in
sharp contrast with the lack of development in Germany. As Clapham wrote, "Germany, quite unlike
France, started the century with an urban life that
was in many ways medieval, and in places less vigor-
ous than it had been in the days of Dürer and Hans
Sachs. . . . The towns managed to grow just a frac-
tion quicker than the population as a whole. Very
many of them were still the quiet little places of the
fairy-books, with huddled roofs and spires, from
which the view over the ploughlands and the
orchards was so easy." From almost every point of
view, except that of philosophic thought, Germany
in the early nineteenth century was undeveloped
compared with France. Not only was Germany
politically retarded, in that there was no unified State
and the Confederation was little but a princely conspiracy for reaction, but also the people were socially
backward to a degree that Germany's subsequent
social development has made us forget. Feudalism
was not overthrown in Prussia until the Stein and
Hardenberg laws of 1807 emancipated the rural
population from serfdom and granted modified freedom in the choice of crafts, but after 1815 reforms
went no further. The old police régime was continued in Prussia, with press-censorship and denial

14

of civil liberties on the eighteenth-century model. The rural population was cowed and the industrial workman seemed satisfied in his misery, happy enough in the hope that he might end his days in no worse a state than he had begun them.

It was no accident that made France the birthplace of socialism. The great Revolution had bred a progeny of ideas and associations which no Bourbon restoration could sterilize. Elsewhere in continental Europe the old ruling families, restored in 1814, held their despotic ground, though shaken in 1830 and 1848, until well into the second half of the century; but in France the Bourbons fell in the July Revolution of 1830 and gave place to Louis-Philippe and the rule of the *grande bourgeoisie*.

*Chapter Two*

# The Young Proudhon

PIERRE-JOSEPH PROUDHON was born at Besançon on 15 January 1809, the eldest child of working-class parents. His father, Claude Proudhon, was a labourer in the cooper's yard of Renaud's brewery, where his mother also worked as a general servant. They lived in a little house in the suburb of Le Battant, the wine-dressers' quarter, huddled between the River Doubs and the ramparts. They were an extremely poor family, but none the less respectable and even respected. Besançon had known priests and lawyers of the name of Proudhon, and a cousin of the brewer's labourer was Professor of Jurisprudence at Dijon. Claude Proudhon, who was illiterate, had no ambitions beyond his station, but his station was not that of the hired labourer. He had bought the house he lived in, and his family, and his wife's family too, owned a few fields out in the country. The Proudhons thought of themselves as their own masters, and it was only to be expected that when the Renaud brewery was pulled down (as part of the plan to clear the town walls for the siege of 1814), Claude should have hung his sign, the Upturned Pot, outside his house in Le Battant and set up for himself as a brewer-publican.

The pot-house did not prosper. Claude Proudhon had his own way of doing business. He would charge for his beer the Just Price : so much for his expenses and so much for his living wage, neither more nor less. Before long the brewing was abandoned, and the father of the young family—there were five children altogether—was making barrels and retailing wine, with long visits to Burgille-en-Marnay, a village some twelve miles west of Besançon where his wife's family lived, for the vine-harvest and the wood-cutting season. He sent his eldest son to work as a cow-herd on the hills at the age of eight.

For nearly five years the boy Proudhon was a cow-herd, and happy as only peasant-lads can be. "What delight," he wrote later, "to roll in the high grass, which I wanted to eat, like my cows; to run barefoot along the wet paths by the hedges, plunging my legs in the wet, soft earth! Often enough on warm June mornings I would take off my clothes and have a dew-bath on the hillside. . . . And the bathing, at every hour of the day, in the river in summer, in the springs in winter! I used to climb trees, explore the caves, catch frogs in the grass and cray-fish in their holes—always terrified of touching a salamander."

It was a solitary life, but well in the tradition of his class. The boy had relatives in most of the villages, and at Burgille everybody knew him. They told him tales of his grandfather, nicknamed Tornési, an ex-soldier of Louis XV's army, who had insisted on exercising his alleged wood-cutting rights in the woods of the lords of Bouffremont and had been imprisoned for his pains. On his release Tornési went calmly back to his wood-cutting. One day, caught by a forest-guard in a clearing, he threw down his axe and killed the forester in fair fight. No one could be found to give evidence against Tornési; the police did not even think it worth while to accuse him of the murder. This story vied with salamanders for first place in the boy's imagination.

By the time he was twelve, Proudhon had begun to develop other interests. The Besançon librarian, M. Weiss, was surprised to find a ragged lad asking confidently for as many as ten books at a session and reading solidly throughout the winter evenings. It was obviously time that he had some schooling. Through the good offices of her old employer, M. Renaud, Madame Proudhon got him a free place as a day-boy at the college at Besançon. Here he was as happy as he had been on the hills, but there were difficulties. His parents had no money to spare for books or clothes. Proudhon went to school capless and bootless. His sabots being too noisy for the wooden floors, he had to leave them in the cloak-room and go into class barefoot. The lack of books was more serious. "I made my Latin studies without a dictionary. When I had translated as much as I could from memory, I left blanks for the words I didn't know and filled them in as soon as I got to school. I was punished a hundred times for having forgotten my books; the fact was, I hadn't got any." Even more serious was the lack of leisure for study. On his free days Proudhon had to work in the fields and help in the house, and during the holidays his job was to comb the woods for withies for his father's barrel-making. Yet somehow or other he got as far as the top class before his father insisted that the time had come for him to earn a living. He became a printer's apprentice in the Besançon firm of Gauthier Brothers.

It was typical of Proudhon that he used the printer's shop as a continuation of his academic studies. The firm specialized in editions of the Bible, the Christian Fathers and in general theological publications. Proudhon, now a printer's reader and compositor, perfected his Latin, learned Hebrew and soaked himself in the Old Testament, in the original and in the Vulgate translation. Thus developed his first two intellectual passions—comparative grammar and theology. Like Renan, he was a philologist and Bible student before he turned to philosophy. His reading, chosen from the patristic works that found their way into the printer's shop, excited him as much as the novels which make up the diet of the average adolescent. He identified himself with each new heresy as the ordinary reader does with each new hero. Arian, Manichean, Pelagian, Gnostic, Adamite, he knew and loved them all, until at last he found, to his despair, that he was a Socinian. Then came a new delight, the works of Bossuet and Fénelon. He wrote with justifiable pride : "I learned the laws of reasoning and style at the hands of the great masters."

There cannot have been many boys who have made better use of a printer's apprenticeship. Michelet, another poor man's son, went through the same literary training, but Michelet had the advantage of an intellectual father. Proudhon had nothing behind him but the barrel-maker's home. There was no one he could turn to for guidance, no one to advise him in his reading, no one with whom he could discuss the ideas that had set his mind on fire. All around him at Besançon were learned and scholarly men, from the forty members of the Besançon Academy to the priests and professors who swarmed in the city; for Besançon was a great provincial centre of culture in those days before Paris had completed the monopoly of the intellectuals of France. But Proud-

hon did not know them, and it is not strange that
they should not have noticed him. (Not until later
did M. Weiss remember the urchin who had pored
over his books in the lamp-lit library.) In the very
suburb of Le Battant where he lived, Fourier had
been born, and there must have been a tradition of
Utopian Socialism or Phalansterianism, as Fourier's
doctrine was known at the time, somewhere in the
neighbourhood. Fourier's disciple, Considérant, also
came from Besançon and was almost Proudhon's
contemporary, but Considérant had gone to Paris.
Courbet the painter, who later became a disciple of
Proudhon, was certainly still in Besançon, but the
ten years by which he was junior to Proudhon must
have been more than enough to prevent their
acquaintance. In any case, Proudhon knew nobody
with whom he could discuss ideas. At the time of
life when intellectual fellowship is most needed—the
normal undergraduate years—Proudhon was alone.

He was over twenty years old before he met a
kindred spirit. Gustave Fallot was a few years older
than Proudhon and almost as poor. He was completing an edition of the Life of the Saints, in Latin, for
Gauthier's, and was surprised to find his careful copy
returned with new and obviously justified correc-
tions. Naturally enough, he sought out the learned
printer's reader, and from this a friendship sprang
up which became the most important thing in the
lives of both young men. Like Proudhon, Fallot was
a born scholar and an impassioned grammarian and
philosopher. It was a disaster for each of them when,
in the middle of 1831, Fallot had to leave Besançon
for Paris. Proudhon's only lifeline was his friendship
with Fallot, to whom he wrote asking if there wasn't
someone in Paris who might want a tutor for his

children. Fallot replied that there was—he knew of one himself—but that a baby-minding job would never do for a free spirit like Proudhon.

He had taken Proudhon's measure. In December 1831 he wrote to him as follows : "For the first time in my life, I am going to risk predicting the future. Keep this letter : re-read it fifteen or twenty years hence—twenty-five years, perhaps—and if the prediction I am about to make has not then been realized, burn it, out of charity and in respect for my memory, as the letter of a madman. This is what I prophesy : You, Proudhon, in spite of yourself and inevitably, by the nature of your destiny, will be a writer, an author; you will be a philosopher; you will be one of the lights of the century and your name will hold its place among those of the nineteenth century as the names of Gassendi, Descartes, Malebranche and Bacon in the seventeenth century, as those of Diderot, Montesquieu, Helvétius, Locke, Hume and Holbach in the eighteenth. Such will be your lot ! Now go and do what you will—set up type, bring up brats, bury yourself in the most obscure and distant villages—it is all the same to me. You will not be able to escape your destiny."

Such prophecies rarely come true, but they never fail to put heart into the recipient. Proudhon walked from Besançon to Paris, making wonderful plans for the life that he and Fallot were going to live together. They were both penniless, but he would get odd jobs as a printer while Fallot would work on his essay for the Suard Prize, a research scholarship which a Madame Suard had endowed at the Besançon Academy; it was to the value of 1,500 francs for three years, and left the recipient free to live where he would and to pursue his own researches. With the

Suard Prize in Fallot's hands, together they would scale the heights of the philosophical Parnassus.

But when Proudhon at last arrived at Fallot's lodging in the rue Mazarin, in March 1832, he found his friend down with cholera and had to nurse him through a long and terrible illness. The Suard Scholarship, which in time was indeed to go to Fallot, had not yet been awarded, and meanwhile the wolf was at the door. Proudhon could not find work. He understood nothing of the revolutionary troubles of Paris, nothing of the journalists' protestation or of the uprising of students and artisans who built barricades, led the rising of the July Days of 1830 and overthrew the Bourbon Monarchy in order to establish Louis-Philippe as constitutional King of France. He understood nothing except that it was all very bad for trade and meant unemployment everywhere, particularly in the printing shops. Nowhere could Proudhon find work. He had to leave Fallot to get through convalescence unattended while he set out on his travels once more. The two friends never met again, for Fallot died shortly after at the age of twenty-nine.

In the summer of 1832 Proudhon made his *tour de France*. It was the custom of the printing trade in those days that the young man who was nearing the end of his apprenticeship should set out on his travels from town to town until he had learned the practice of the trade in various parts, had earned the good report of many masters and was equipped to establish himself in his profession. The custom had once applied to nearly all apprenticeships, and although it was now dying out in most trades, the Companions of the Tour of France, with their customary clothes, their scrip and their staves, were still familiar figures on the roads, still had their recognized houses for lodging and a sort of masonic guild, with secret signs and catch-words, for their organization.

Proudhon was not happy on his tour. "In order to live, I had to leave my town and my native districts, had to take the costume and staff of a Companion of the Tour of France, and to go from printer's shop to printer's shop, seeking here a few lines to set up, there a few proof-sheets to read. One day I sold my school prizes, the only library I had ever possessed. My mother wept when she heard of it, but I still had the manuscript notes that I had copied out of the books." He began by going to Neufchâtel and worked his way round on foot to Lyons, Marseilles, Toulon and Draguignon. At Toulon he could find neither work nor lodging and came near to starvation. He was abominably lonely and was despairing of his future as a printer.

Back in Besançon and worn out with journey-man's work, Proudhon had the idea of setting up a shop of his own in partnership with two colleagues, Lambert and Maurice. They had only a few pounds saved between them, but Lambert's family had a little capital and Proudhon got his father to pledge his meagre credit up to the last penny. The partners worked like galley-slaves and lived on crusts, but profitable business did not come their way and, before Proudhon realized what was happening, they were deep in debt. Lambert realized it only too well. One day he disappeared, to be found a month later in a corner of a wood, dead by his own hand. Proudhon was now not only friendless and penniless, but solely responsible for the printer's shop and saddled with the whole debt of the establishment.

It was fortunate for Proudhon, and for posterity,

that a serious illness kept him in bed throughout the winter of 1836–7, forcing him to postpone any attempt to earn a living and leaving him to live his own life, the life of ideas. They were not at this time political ideas. "By my personal tastes I am entirely foreign to the debates and quarrels of politics," he wrote to a local newspaper proprietor who had invited his collaboration. "What benefit could you extract, Monsieur, from a man whose life has been taken up with the study of languages, metaphysics and theology?" But he went on to add a piece of characteristic advice : "Why not invite people to make themselves capable of managing their own affairs? Let them seek, through education, science, sound morals and patriotism, to do without all ministerial and constitutional hierarchies."

Proudhon was working on an *Essaie de Grammaire Générale* in which, he said, he would describe the principles from which "would be deducted one day in demonstrable fashion, by comparative philology, the period at which mankind first began to speak, and consequently the age of humanity, and relationship of the human families, and the place of the cradle of the human race."

When he recovered he hastened to print this *Essaie*, and on the strength of it made his application to the Besançon Academy for the Suard Scholarship. "To seek psychology in new regions, philosophy by new roads; to study the nature and mechanism of the human spirit in the most apparent and tangible of its manifestations—in speech; to determine, from the origin and processes of language, the source and relationship of human creeds; to apply, in a word, grammar to metaphysics and ethics, and to follow out the idea which worries the most profound geniuses, and which preoccupied Fallot and still pre-occupies Pauthier [the two previous recipients of the Suard award]—such, Messieurs, is the task which I would impose on myself if you were to accord me the books and the time. Above all, the books. I shall never lack the time."

But it was not only as a scholar that Proudhon solicited the Suard bursary. He appended to his formal letter of application a paragraph so outrageously original that it almost lost him the award. "Born and bred in the bosom of the working-class, belonging to it still in my heart and affections and above all in common suffering and aspirations, my greatest joy, if I were to win your votes, would assuredly be, Messieurs, to be enabled henceforth to work without cease, through science and philosophy, with all the energy of my will and all the powers of my spirit, for the betterment, moral and intellectual, of those whom I delight to call my brothers and my companions, to be able to propagate among them the seeds of a doctrine which I regard as the moral law of the world; and, while awaiting the success of my efforts, to find myself at the same time, under your wise guidance, their representative at your Academy."

It says much for the Besançon Academicians that in spite of this profession of revolutionary faith they gave Proudhon the Suard Scholarship. It says even more for them that they did not withdraw it after the first year. All the reports that reached them from Paris showed that their protégé was not settling down. Proudhon was indeed calling regularly on his appointed tutor, M. Droz, but he refused all the old gentleman's advice and declined to follow any orthodox line of research. He had nothing but scorn for the crowned heads of Parisian scholarship. After a single visit to the lecture-rooms of Victor Cousin, Jouffroy, Damiron and Cardaillac, he gave them up as a pack of back-scratchers and windbags—a verdict which he would revise in later years. The lectures of Michelet, Rossi, Lenormand and Saint-Marc-Girardin he followed at greater length, only to conclude that "they all seemed to extol the blessing of the constitutional régime and to preach the most centralizing form of centralization." His head was buzzing with ideas on every subject under the sun, but he belonged to no social hive; he was reading voraciously and had a clear though undefined sense of a mission, but it was not one that would fit into any academic or professional category; he was an uncouth provincial, and there was no one in Paris whom he could talk with. In Besançon he had made friends with two Alsatian scholars who had begun to take the place of Fallot in his life; but of these one, Bergmann, was in Strasbourg and the other, Ackermann, had gone to Berlin to take on a seven-years' job editing the papers of Frederick the Great. Solitude was beginning to make Proudhon feel eccentric, even to himself. "Mine is a difficult nature—a morose, defiant, stormy, misanthropic nature," he wrote to the Secretary of Besançon Academy. "M. Droz has already realized it, and the upshot of our conversation is that no sort of career is likely to be accessible to me."

What sort of career could be open to such an uncompromising man? The nearest that Proudhon could get to a project at that time—it was 1839 and he was thirty years old—was to be found in the *Revue du Franche-Comté*, which would make his compatriots conscious of their culture, proud of their

26

local traditions and of their individuality. Society was still meaningless to Proudhon except in terms of his native region. Paris he loathed—and characterized in a string of Hobbesian epithets : beastly, filthy, boastful, egoistic, proud and duped. He felt himself a Besançon man and as such a citizen of no mean city. His emotions were centred in the Franche-Comté, which he called not only his native home but his country and even his nation. "I suffer from my exile," he wrote from Paris in 1839. "I detest Parisian civilization, and cry to whomever has ears : *Fugite de medio Babylonis.* I shall never have peace, I shall never recover the use of my mind and faculties, I shall never be able to write except on the banks of the Doubs, the Ognon and the Loue." (It was characteristic of him that he resisted the literary man's temptation to put an adjective to these rivers; he would always resist such temptations.) The Franche-Comté was his country. He would not even call himself a Burgundian. His criticism of the *Revue des Deux Bourgognes* was that it was too much of the Duchy and not enough of the County.

M. Droz could not understand. From a member of the *Académie Française* who voted against Victor Hugo's candidacy, preferring that of Casimir Bonjour, we should hardly expect understanding. But he was not unkind to Proudhon, especially when he discovered one tangible reason for the young man's oddity—Proudhon had no money. Most of the Suard emoluments never left Besançon, where they were ear-marked for the payment of debt arising out of the bankrupt printing establishment. Proudhon was working as a penny-a-liner, grinding out articles on logic and theology for Parent-Desbarres' Encyclopædia. M. Parent-Desbarres extracted 200 francs' worth of articles from Proudhon before the wretched hack discovered that he had no intention of paying. In February 1840 we find Proudhon writing to his friend Bergmann in Strasbourg : "You thought that I was poor last year; this year, if you come to Paris, you will find me indigent. I'll have 250 francs to live on from March 20 to September 20. It's all very well for me to read and write and study; I'm weighed down, hemmed-in, beaten. Sometimes when I cross the bridges, I look at the Seine. Sometimes I think of turning thief. The poverty has made such an impression on me that, if I were to come into a fortune tomorrow, it would still haunt me for a couple of years." (Again, how characteristic that he should avoid writing "for ever"; a couple of years was as far as hyperbole could go.)

All this went far to explain the student's volubility, but nothing could excuse, in M. Droz's eyes, his pupil's first literary efforts. In 1839 Proudhon submitted for a prize competition at Besançon Academy an essay on Sunday Observance. Here the grammarian and theologian began to get social studies into literary focus for the first time. Not content with explaining "how it comes about that a religion can be false while its content is true," Proudhon set about to discover "a state of social equality which is neither community nor despotism, neither unsettlement nor anarchy, but liberty in order and independence in unity." Altogether it was a most disturbing piece of work, and the wonder is that it was deemed worthy of fourth place in the list and a bronze medal. But a thousand times more disturbing was the long pamphlet which Proudhon published by subscription in 1840, without a word to M. Droz and with a totally unauthorized dedication to the members of the Besançon Academy. Its title was a question—"What is Property?—and the answer was given in the first paragraph : "Property is theft."

This became the most famous revolutionary phrase of the nineteenth century. The thesis of the pamphlet—that property, especially in its attributes of profit, rent and interest, which Proudhon called collectively *aubaine*, was the cancer at the heart of society—became the theme-song of generations of agitators. We need to remind ourselves, therefore, that at the time of its publication, and for years after, the pamphlet was not read by the public and hardly noticed by the Press. Only on the members of the Besançon Academy did it have any immediate effect. They were scandalized, very properly, and demanded an explanation. Proudhon wrote to them emphasizing the educational intention of his work, and explaining that the dedication had not been intended to commit his patrons in any way, but merely to express his debt to them as their Suard scholar. He meant the letter to be conciliatory, but none of its recipients, except possibly M. Weiss and M. Pérennès, the Secretary, who were beginning to know their Proudhon, would discern the kind intention behind this sentence : "Your first emotion will pass, and the disturbance which the bold expression of a hitherto unperceived physical and economic truth may have caused in you will calm down; with time and reflection you will come, I am sure, to an enlightened realization of your own sentiments, which now you are ignorant of, which you combat, and which I defend." His next letter was rather more apologetic—"When after thirty years of a life of hard work a man sees himself on the verge of starvation and when he suddenly discovers in a verbal equivocation, in a piece of false accountancy, the cause of the evil which tortures him and millions of his fellows, then it is difficult for him to refrain from uttering a cry of sorrow and of horror"; but he could not refrain, in honesty, from adding: "You are unqualified by sufficient or special research to pronounce a verdict on a theory of Property."

Proudhon's thesis was not nicely argued; as Beaugin pointed out, it was crude, sweeping and pamphleteering in style, but for all that it was a piece of substantial reasoning. Proudhon began by proving that property was not a natural right, since, for one thing, it was denied by legal limitations and by accepted customs such as progressive taxation. "Adored by all, it is recognized by none : law, custom, tradition, public and private conscience all conspire towards its death and ruin." Nor was it a right based on occupation or on labour. In fact, it is an economic contradiction, since the property-owner sells to the worker the worker's own product at a higher price than he pays him for his work. In all this Proudhon was attacking the orthodox economists, but his heaviest blows were reserved for the revolutionaries, for the Utopian Socialists of the schools of Fourier and Saint-Simon. Against them he argued that all salaries should be the same. While admitting the infinite inequality of talent and the hierarchy of function, he insisted on the complete equality of reward. Artists should not be paid more than sweepers : "The artist, the scholar, the poet receive their just reward from the very fact that society permits them to devote themselves exclusively to science and to art." The Besançon Academicians might well feel unable to pronounce on such theories.

Here and there they would recognize echoes in Proudhon's style. Here a piece of Rousseau : "How has the instinct for society, so sure among animal tribes, come to fail in man ? How comes it that man, born for society, is not yet associated?" There a bit of Hegel : "Community [*communauté*] is the first term of social development, the *thesis*; property, the contradiction of community, is the second term, the *antithesis*. It remains to discover the third term, the *synthesis*, and we shall have the solution we seek." But when he called the third term Liberty, they would be lost and frightened. Fourierism they were acquainted with, but this was something new, and the new is always frightening.

Proudhon expected that his bursary would be stopped. In any case, it had only another six months to run. He began to look round for a way of earning his living, and found a county-court judge who wanted a collaborator for a book he was writing on Preventive Punishment. The judge offered him 150 francs a month and his keep in return for the book. The would-be author had no intellectual or literary ability, and indeed no interest in the subject; he merely wanted something of a progressive nature to be published in his name so that he might become known as a promising candidate for Parliament. Proudhon accepted, and rather enjoyed his legal devilling. Meanwhile the Besançon Academy, somewhat reassured by a testimonial from Louis Blanc, then Professor at the *Collège de France*, refrained from cutting short the term of the bursary. But they had not heard the last of Proudhon. In 1841 he was at work on a second essay on property, dedicated this time to Blanqui, and in January 1842 a third essay appeared under the title of *Avertissement aux*

*Propriétaires, ou Lettre à M. Considérant.* The second pamphlet was almost moderate in tone, but the third was not. Proudhon was hitting about in all directions, and the powers-that-be had had enough. Eight days after publication, the *Avertissement* was seized, and in February the author was summoned to appear before the Doubs Assizes on a charge of conspiracy against the social order.

We must pause a moment at this crisis and ask ourselves what Proudhon was about. He was thirty-three now, and conscious not only of his mission but of his limitations and what it would cost. In 1840 he had written to Ackermann: "Since Rousseau wrote the profession of faith of the *Vicaire Savoyard*, no man has perhaps had a clearer consciousness of the truth of his writing, and none a more profound sadness than mine." A year later he was writing to Antoine Gauthier: "All the same, this progressive abolition of property would only be the *negation of an evil* not a *positive organization.* As for that, my dear friend, I can certainly outline the principles and the general laws, but I cannot undertake all the details. That would be a work to absorb fifty Montesquieus. For my part, I can lay down the axioms; I can provide examples and a method; I can get the thing *going.* It's for everyone else to do the rest. And be sure of this: no one on earth is capable, as Saint-Simon and Fourier have pretended, of drawing up a system, complete in all parts, which needs nothing but to be put in motion. That is the most damnable lie that could be presented to mankind."

It is interesting to compare his career with that of Michelet, whose experience and aspiration was so close to Proudhon's own. Michelet, too, had suffered from poverty at school; he, too, had lost his only

friend in circumstances much the same as those
which had killed Fallot; he, too, was consumed with
a passion for scholarship and with an acute sense of
his mission and of its cost. In a letter written in 1831
—when he was thirty-three—he said: "I believe
I have found through concentration and retrospec-
tion, a flame sufficiently intense to melt down all the
apparent diversities, to restore to them in history the
unity they had in life. To undertake to combine so
many different elements alien to one another is to
harbour in oneself a great disturbing force. To re-
produce so many passions is not to calm one's own.
A lamp which is hot enough to fuse whole people is
hot enough to consume its very hearth." But Michelet's path lay in pleasant places. He became tutor to
the Princesse de Parme at the Tuileries, and as a
very young man was professor at the Collège de
Paris. Proudhon's literary apprenticeship had included seven years of schooling, ten years in and out
of printing-works, three years of study in Paris. He
had never been free from financial worry, and he
had never had quite enough to eat. The only regular
employment he had found was as ghost-writer to a
lawyer; the only public recognition was that now
afforded him by the public prosecutor at Doubs.

The Doubs Assizes provided an unexpected piece
of comedy. Proudhon had never appeared in public
before. The court was crowded with the leaders of
Besançon society, agog for the sight of a revolutionary at bay. They expected to see a rustic rebel goaded
by counsel's sarcasm into roaring insurrectionary
slogans. What they saw was an intellectual, lean and
heavily built, with a head so massive that it seemed
to make him stoop. A domed forehead pressed
heavily over brown eyes in which close observers

noted a slight cast. The broadness of the face, with its blunt features and bellicose upper lip, was underlined by a fringe of beard. What they heard was a polite voice inflicting on the court a discourse so erudite and incomprehensible that the judges were baffled and put out of countenance. There was nothing they could do but acquit the young man who had treated their court as a professor might treat pupils in a familiar lecture-room.

No one appreciated this comedy better than the leading actor. "Imagine," Proudhon wrote to Ackermann, "the astonishment of all those inquisitive people—priests, ladies, gentry and so on—when, instead of a red-waistcoated, goat-bearded, sepulchral-voiced Republican, they saw a little fair man with a calm expression and amiable, straightforward manner, explaining that the charge against him was based on a mistake on the part of the bar—for whose zeal, incidentally, he had nothing but praise—and affirming that his ideas were those of everybody and that, far from being hostile to the government, they were most favourable to it . . . and proving this thesis by scientific arguments so abstruse, so difficult to follow and couched in terms varying from an extreme clarity and simplicity to metaphysical and technological profundity that the court ended by understanding nothing at all. Imagine, I say, a man accused of conspiracy against the social order putting forward in his defence a stew of political economy so hard to digest or get hold of that everyone admitted that it meant nothing to them—then you'll have some idea of the judges' mystification." They pronounced Proudhon "an economist, not an anarchist; a man of meditation, not of revolution," and acquitted him. "It is for me to conserve this magnificent position," he wrote triumphantly to Bergmann.

In mystifying his judges Proudhon had to some extent mystified himself. He really believed that he was a mild little man who wanted nothing more than some steady clerical job which would earn him leisure to pursue his studies in peace. He began applying for minor posts in the local government offices, and was naïvely surprised when he was refused. Certainly he had every reason to worry about the future. He had just succeeded in selling his printing-shop, but at a price which did not nearly cover the debts; he was left with a 7,000-franc deficit to pay off in annual instalments. "Turned down by the Prefecture and by the City Hall, suspect to the police, hated by the clergy, feared by the bourgeois. Now, without profession, without possessions and without credit— that's where I've got to at the age of thirty-four." At last he was offered a job by his old patrons, the Gauthiers, who ran a haulage company in the waterways round Lyons.

"Oh, the dirty city !" wrote Proudhon to Maurice a few weeks after his arrival. "Since I came to Lyons I have taken to wearing spectacles, and I wish I hadn't. Before, all the women looked passable; now they look atrocious. At first I blamed my glasses, but one day when I was in the museum I recognized that all the beautiful things really did look very beautiful, and all the ugly ones uglier than ever." To Ackermann he wrote in September 1944 : "I'm a waterman's clerk in Lyons. I pass my days with bargees, draymen and dockers, with business-men, commercial travellers, coalheavers, etc., sometimes in my office, sometimes aboard our tug, the Dragon." Unpromising as the work sounded, Proudhon turned it to excellent account. He could never be other than conscientious and contentious, and the firm did well to put him in charge of their litigation. For his part, Proudhon learned a great deal of applied economics, developed views about public transport and company finance, and enjoyed, as theoreticians always do, the enforced preoccupation with practical problems. "I am accumulating evidence," he went on in his letter to Ackermann, "completing *ab experto* the course in political economy which I began as a student of Adam Smith and Say ... My time will not be wasted; after having been an industrialist ruined by competition, I am contributing in my turn to the ruin of others. You can't imagine the appalling effect of a learned theory applied destructively."

It did not need the perspicacity of a Proudhon to see how the wealth of nations pursued through free trade and competition was degrading the workers of France at this stage of the industrial revolution. In the newly opened mines (the number of miners increased from 15,600 in 1831 to 35,000 in 1847) conditions were monstrous. In the spinning-mills children of four and five years old were working the same hours as adults (an enquiry of 1840–5 showed that in 63 Departments of France 131,098 children and 254,871 women were employed; together they outnumbered the men workers). It was a recognized fact that everywhere the little men were being driven out of business by the big employers. "The incursion of monopoly into commerce and industry is too well known for it to be necessary for me to quote the evidence," wrote Proudhon in 1844.

The year 1843 saw the publication of *De la création de l'Ordre dans l'Humanité, ou Principes d'Organization politique*. It was Proudhon's most disappointing book, full of undigested ideas and unrelated theories, interesting to the student for the development of notions that had appeared in earlier works and for the first appearance of notions, such as the theory of surplus value, which would be developed later, but hardly significant in itself. Proudhon himself came to regret its publication: "I wanted to make an analysis of society, but I knew nothing about it." His next book was immeasurably better. For three years while employed by the Gauthiers, in Lyons and occasionally in Paris, he wrestled with the problem presented by the contradiction between the degrading effects of competition and of the division of labour and the no less obvious fact that those methods of economic organization were the ineluctable conditions of economic progress and of social equality itself. Gradually he began to see a mode of thought which would reconcile the contradiction. His whole cast of mind was deductive : he always argued from the general to the particular, from God to Man, from metaphysics to economics, "which are but the external realization of the former, as phenomena are of numena." He began now to develop his thought in terms of thesis, antithesis and synthesis. Such systematic thinking did not altogether suit him. The motto of the book was to be *Destruam et Ædificabo*, but the new edifice was not yet in sight.

*Chapter Three*

# The Young Marx

KARL MARX was born in the Rhineland town of Trier on 5 May 1818, the second surviving child of bourgeois Jewish parents. It was a rabbinical family. His grandfather, Marx Levi (a name which became abbreviated to Marx) was rabbi of Trier, and married into a family whose ancestors included distinguished rabbis as far back as the sixteenth century. Marx Levi's eldest son succeeded him as rabbi of Trier, and if his youngest, Herschel Marx, who was to be Karl's father, took law as his profession, he too married into a rabbinical family. Karl's mother, Henriette Presborck, came of a family as famous for its rabbis as his paternal grandmother's.

Herschel Marx was a child of his generation. The whole intellectual climate of the Rhineland had been changed by the incursion of the French revolutionary armies. Western winds had freshened the sultry streets of the medieval cities, and when Napoleon made Trier part of the Confederation of the Rhine a new age opened not only for Germans but for Jews. The barriers which for centuries had separated Jews from Germans were swept away; trades and professions which had been traditionally closed to Jews were opened to them. Herschel Marx felt himself as much a German as a Jew, and perhaps more a child of the Enlightenment than either. He was a disciple of Lessing and Kant, and one of his granddaughters recalled the impression that he knew his Voltaire and Rousseau by heart.

The fall of Napoleon was followed, not by the establishment of a liberal united Germany as Herschel Marx had expected, but by the restoration of the old petty monarchies and principalities with the old sequestration of the Jews. Trier was incorporated in the Prussian Kingdom, and the Prussian régime under Frederick William III was racially reactionary. Prussian laws banned non-Christians from State service and from the liberal professions, and Herschel Marx was a lawyer attached to the Court. His choice now lay between changing either his faith or his profession. He had no hesitation : he took the Christian name of Heinrich and was received into the Evangelical Established Church of the Prussian Kingdom in 1817. His wife could not follow him in this. She was not a German Jewess—her family had come from Hungary—and the intellectual climate of the West meant nothing to her. At first she refused baptism for herself, but could not refuse it to her children.

Karl Marx was thus a Jew and not a Jew, a Christian and not a Christian, a Prussian and not a Prussian. These contradictions meant much to him in later life, but in his early years they meant nothing at all. It was a happy family, the mother immersed in the care of household and children (there were to be eight of them), the eldest daughter and son, Sophie and Karl, close and affectionate companions, the father socially accepted and moderately successful, exercising in his home the authority which is the privilege of heads of Jewish households and the respectful tolerance that is the pride of liberal humanists. There can have been few happier relationships between father and son than that between Heinrich and Karl Marx. There was admiration and confidence between them as well as love, and as the boy grew up he acquired his father's literary and philosophical interests. At Trier Gymnasium (Grammar School), where he went at the age of twelve, he did well in literary subjects and less well in theology. His masters found him an earnest, industrious lad, not highly distinguished, and there was little in the schoolboy to foreshadow the adult Marx, unless we count an essay in his leaving examination on Choosing a Profession, in which he wrote : "But we cannot always follow the profession to which we feel ourselves to be called; our relationships in society have already to some extent been formed before we are in a position to determine them."

Neither his father nor his school were the main influences on Marx as a boy. He found a guide, philosopher and friend in Freiherr Ludwig von Westphalen, whose house was in the same street as the Marxs's and in whose garden Sophie and Karl used to play. They were a strange couple, the middle-aged aristocrat and the little Jewish boy, but they had interests in common which few of the other 11,000 inhabitants of Trier could share—a delight, for instance, in Homer and the Greek dramatists and in Shakespeare, and a taste for discussing the literature of half a dozen languages while they strolled on the hills of the Mosel. It was from Ludwig von Westphalen that Marx first learnt of Saint-Simon.

When he was seventeen Marx went to the University of Bonn where he spent a delightful year. He did little work. Nominally he was reading law, but the lectures he preferred were Schlegel's on Homer, and his reading was mostly on mythology and poetry. He spent a lot of money, got himself arrested for "nocturnal noisiness and drunkenness," and ended by fighting a duel in which he was wounded over the eye. Altogether it was a very typical first year for a spirited undergraduate.

When he came home for the summer there was a shock for his family and, we imagine, for Freiherr von Westphalen. He asked their consent for his engagement to Jenny von Westphalen, the Freiherr's daughter. There seemed to be everything against the match. Karl was eighteen, Jenny was twenty-two and the prettiest, most sought-after girl in the town. There could be no question of marriage for years, until Karl had completed his education and had entered on a career. Karl was a middle-class boy, the grandchild of rabbis; Jenny an aristocrat whose grandfather had been adviser to the Duke of Brunswick and whose grandmother was a Wishart, related to the Duke of Argyle's family. It says much for the Freiherr's feeling for Karl Marx that he gave his consent without demur. Heinrich Marx was more apprehensive; he knew that the boy had been in love with Jenny for twelve months or more, but he also knew that being in love was not enough. He refused to let Karl return to Bonn, which was altogether too near to Trier, and sent him to the University of Berlin.

With the journey to Berlin, Karl Marx found himself plunged into a new world. He had had the most provincial of boyhoods—in Trier the oldest and almost the sleepiest of German towns, where gas-lighting was still unknown and the wonder of the day was the first railway train and the first steamboat on the Mosel, and in Bonn which for all its intellectual activity was still eighteenth-century in outlook and atmosphere. Berlin was new and feverish and crowded, a metropolis of 320,000 inhabitants, the biggest of German towns after Vienna. Marx rented a room in the Leipzigerstrasse, in the house where Lessing had lived, and tried to find his feet. He was very lonely, and somehow he found it impossible to do any work. He was supposed to be reading law, but it bored him and soon he dropped all lecture courses except the minimum which law students were obliged to attend. The first year passed in multifarious, undirected reading and in writing poems for Jenny. They were bad poems, as he was ready to admit in a letter written only a year later: "Feeling flat and formless; nothing natural about them; everything up in the air; utter contradiction between what is and what should be; rhetorical reflections instead of poetic ideas."

His father was vastly worried. He trusted his son and believed in his genius, but what he heard of his life in Berlin was not encouraging. "God help us," he wrote to Karl, "lack of order, a brooding prowling-around in all the fields of science, a stuffy brooding under a dismal oil-lamp. Going to seed in a scholastic dressing-gown with unkempt hair as a change from going to seed with beer-glass in hand. Repellent unsociability and the consignment of everything decent, even consideration for your own father, to a secondary position. The limitation of the social art to a dirty room where in woeful disorder the love-letter of a Jenny and the well-meaning exhortations of a father, written with tears perhaps, are used as pipe-lighters—which, by the way, is better than that they should fall into the hands of third persons as the result of a still more irresponsible disorder."

When Karl Marx was in his second year in Berlin his father died. It was the first serious blow he had

had to bear, and it left him rootless. His interests
turned away from literature, which had been his
father's passion, and focused on philosophy, a study
which absorbed him to the exclusion of all else for
the next three years. In the Germany of that time
philosophy meant Hegel and the home of Hegelianism was Berlin. Hegelianism meant an end to thinking of history as a chapter of accidents or as a collection of unconnected stories; it meant the beginning
of thinking of it as an organic process of the working
of the spirit. But this process was not smoothly continuous; it was the result of conflict, one force being
confronted by its opposite, and the struggle anni-
hilating each and leading to a third force which
transcends both. It was this Hegelian dialectic,
thesis-antithesis-synthesis, that fascinated the young
Marx, a fascination strong enough to remain with
him to the end of his days.

He studied Hegel independently, devouring his
books day and night, and taking no notice of the
University lectures on the subject. At the instance of
the Prussian Government, the University of Berlin
had made Hegelianism an official cult (had not
Hegel said that the State "represents the highest law
for the individual, whose highest duty is to be a
member of the State"?), and a very tiresome cult it
had become. There was a revolt against it led by
men who called themselves Young Hegelians and organized in a periodical called the *Hallische Jahrbücher*. This was not a review but a solid volume,
as it had to be, for all newspapers and periodical re-
views were subject to the Prussian censorship from
which only books of 320 pages or more were exempt.
Its contributors were mostly the Young Hegelians of
Berlin. Marx was strongly attracted to them, and

spent the better part of three years in a beer-cellar where their club used to meet. He was younger than the others—a boy of twenty while they were men in their thirties—but somehow or other, perhaps by his capacity for philosophical argument, perhaps by his single-mindedness, he established a sort of ascendancy over them. Koppen, the revolutionary historian, dedicated a book to "my friend Karl Marx of Trier." Bruno Bauer, the theologian who denied the historical evidence of the Gospels, admired him enough to want to join Marx's career with his; when Bauer was sent as a lecturer to Bonn with a view to succeeding the professor there, his idea was that Marx should follow as a lecturer in his faculty, and that between them they should revolutionize the thinking of Bonn.

Before Marx could hold a university appointment he must have a degree, and before he could have a degree he must write a dissertation. There were two difficulties about this. One was the personal difficulty, which Marx never got over, of committing his ideas quickly to paper in a form which would satisfy him as worthy of publication; the other was the political difficulty of getting anything in the least unorthodox accepted by the University of Berlin, which was falling more and more under the control of a reactionary Government alarmed at the dangerous thoughts of the Young Hegelians. It was 1840 before Marx had finished his dissertation (on the philosophy of Democritus and Epicurus), and then he decided to submit it, not to the University of Berlin but to that of Jena. Standards were lower and conditions freer at Jena : one had simply to send one's thesis by post, and in due course, without *viva-voce* examination, one would receive a doctorate.

Thus Marx became a Doctor of Philosophy of the University of Jena. But no academic career was to follow. The Prussian Government had got on the tracks of Bruno Bauer, who had had to surrender his appointment at Bonn in October 1841, a few months after Marx had left Berlin to join him. Marx had been a university student for nearly six years and engaged to be married for five, and he still had no prospect of being able to earn his living or to marry Jenny. He was not, however, dispirited. He was full of schemes for collaborating with Bauer in a review to be called the Archives of Atheism. In a letter to a brother, Bruno Bauer described a day in the country with Marx in the spring of 1842 : "We were as usual very gay. At Godesberg we hired a couple of donkeys and galloped them round the hill and through the village. The good burghers of Bonn who happened to be there looked at us with expressions more scandalized than ever. We were letting out shouts of joy, to which the donkeys replied by braying." Their holidays were happier than their literary collaboration, to which, in spite of promises, Marx contributed nothing. His only finished work besides his doctorate thesis was an attack on the censorship which he sent to Ruge for his *Deutsche Jahrbücher*, and which because of that very censorship Ruge could not print.

Luckily for Marx, there was another patron. Moses Hess, the son of a Rhineland business-man, had met him among the Young Hegelians and had been inordinately impressed. In a letter to a friend, Hess called him "the greatest, actually the only true philosopher now living; soon, when he has shown himself in public through his writings and lectures, he will draw the attention of all Germany. . . . He is a very young man, twenty-four years old at the most, who will give the *coup de grâce* to our medieval religion and politics." Moses Hess had lived in Paris and soaked himself in Babeuf, Saint-Simon and Fourier, and the little book which he published on his return to Bonn in 1837 was almost the first expression of socialist thought in Germany. His second book, the *European Triarchy*, published in 1841, emphasized that the problem of the day was not political but social—it did not lie in the deprivation of political rights, but in the exploitation of the people by a new aristocracy, the aristocracy of money. He had converted a number of young Germans, including Friedrich Engels, to this view. His idea now was to found a radical newspaper in the Rhineland. Through his family's commercial connections he was able to induce a group of respectable business-men in Cologne to finance a paper called the *Rheinische Zeitung*. Their idea was to promote the interests of the Rhineland business community by attacking free trade, the extension of State railways and other forms of economic unification. It was meant to be a moderately liberal rather than a tendentiously radical paper, but the young barristers to whom they entrusted the editorship were full of Young Hegelian ideas and soon went too far for the proprietors' taste. A new editor-in-chief was needed, and their choice fell, very surprisingly, on Karl Marx, a quite unknown young man whose first printed work had been an article against State censorship, which he had sent to the *Zeitung* five months late. How Hess engineered this appointment is not known.

A more exciting task than the editing of a newspaper can hardly be imagined for a young man of twenty-four. Marx conducted it with all the wariness of the middle-aged. He cut out contributions from the Berlin Young Hegelians whose militant atheism was asking for trouble. He showed the greatest skill in dealing with the very stupid censors whom the Berlin Government sent to the Rhineland. He kept the paper firmly on the course of the liberal bourgeoisie, whose enemies were clericalism and the feudalism of the landowners who controlled the Rhineland Diet. Among his own contributions was a passionate defence of the poor man's right to gather sticks in the landowners' forests. There was no socialism in the paper—Marx was not yet a socialist. It was a liberal journal, and its end came through an indiscretion by Marx for which no liberal could have blamed him. In a series of editorials he had attacked the Russian Government as the citadel of reaction which everyone recognized it to be. The paper happened to come to the notice of the Csar, who reproached his ally, the Prussian King, for the slackness of his censors. The Prussian Government thereupon obligingly suppressed the *Rheinische Zeitung*.

On his twenty-fifth birthday Marx was back in Trier, unemployed and, as far as a career in Germany was concerned, virtually unemployable. He had the meagrest academic qualifications and, lacking a patron in university circles, no prospect of an academic career. He was known in the Rhineland as a dangerously liberal journalist whom the censors were not likely to spare in the future. Marx was undismayed by all this: "It is bad to work for freedom in servitude," he wrote in a letter at this time, "and to fight with pens instead of clubs. I am sick of the hypocrisy, the stupidity, the brutal authority, and of our cringing and complying and quibbling and our tergiversation. And now the Government has given me back my freedom. . . . There is in Germany no

47

possible career for me." The only work that offered itself was collaboration with a Saxon journalist, Arnold Ruge, who was founding a periodical to be called the *Deutsch-Französische Jahrbücher* to bring together the best radical thought of Germany and France.

This seemed enough to make marriage possible. Marx and Jenny had been engaged for over seven years and, since the death of their fathers, family opposition had been growing stronger and stronger. A dowry for Jenny and an allowance for Marx seemed out of the question. They were married in April 1843, and after living for a few months in the Westphalens' house, they packed up a few possessions and set out for Paris, where Marx was to edit the *Deutsch-Französische Jahrbücher*.

It was an unpropitious start to what was to be the happiest of marriages. Not many love affairs have survived seven years of engagement; still fewer have survived the sort of strain which Marx put on Jenny during their married life. Perhaps the most remarkable thing about Karl Marx is his extraordinary success in the personal relationships that matter most. His relationship with his father had been satisfying in a way that few such relationships can be. The friendship of Jenny's father, Ludwig von Westphalen, had given him a self-confidence which nothing could shake. Jenny's love for him and his for her was to suffer no rift from his eighteenth year to her death forty-six years later. Already at the age of twenty-five he had all the emotional sustenance, all the love, affection and admiration, that his nature needed. For the rest of his life he made no new personal relationships, except with his children who adored him and with Friedrich Engels in whom he found a friend of his own age who would support him in more senses than one through every vicissitude. He could afford to quarrel with everyone else in the world, to betray patrons, to refuse partners, to vituperate against allies, to belabour colleagues and bully disciples. Some people would say that his happy family relationships had spoiled him; others that they had made him capable of doing great work.

When he went to Paris with Jenny in the autumn of 1843 his life's work had not begun. He was not a socialist and he had never met anyone who was, unless we count the volatile Moses Hess. He was not interested in the working-class and was not conscious of having met anyone who belonged to it. Apart from his four months in Cologne, he had led a singularly secluded life. The society in which his family lived in Trier was a tiny community of Lutheran officials, cut off by their religion from the rest of the citizens, who were almost all Catholics. In Bonn and in Berlin he had not moved outside a very narrow circle of students and teachers. His education from books had been wide enough—he was a most voracious and retentive reader—but his thought had reached a point when it needed a new stimulus.

*Chapter Four*

# They Meet

THE purpose for which Marx and Ruge had come
to Paris and for which the *Deutsch-Französische
Jahrbücher* was intended was to bring together the
radical philosophic thought of France and Germany.
There could be no better time and place for this than
the Paris of the decade before 1848. Perhaps more
than at any other time Paris was the cultural capital
of the world. For most of continental Europe it was
the age of Metternich, an age of censorship and repression; but for Paris, as Isaiah Berlin wrote in his
book on Marx, "it was a decade during which a
richer international traffic in ideas, theories, personal
sentiments, was carried on than during any previous
period; there were alive at this time, congregated in
the same place, attracting, repelling and transform-
ing each other, men of gifts more varied, more striking and more articulate than at any time since the
Renaissance. Every year brought new exiles from the
territories of the Emperor and the Czar. Italian,
Polish, Hungarian, Russian, German colonies throve
in the atmosphere of universal sympathy and admiration. Their members founded international
committees, wrote pamphlets, addressed assemblies,
entered conspiracies, but above all talked and argued
ceaselessly in private houses, in the streets, in cafés, at

public banquets; the mood was exalted and optimistic."

It did not take Marx long to meet the German colony in Paris. No fewer than 85,000 Germans were there in 1843, including a large number of political refugees. Most of them were skilled artisans plying their trades by day and meeting for discussion in the evening. In those circles Marx met working-class socialists for the first time. He did not form a very favourable opinion of them. But after all, he had not gone to France to meet Germans, not even great Germans like the poet Heine. He was already in touch with all the German writers he needed: Jacoby, Moses Hess and Feuerbach would all write for the first number of the *Jahrbücher*. What he needed was French contributors, and there a difficulty arose.

It was a great age of French radical thought, and socialism was becoming almost fashionable in Parisian literary circles. In the four years before 1843 no fewer than eight writers had published striking attacks on the capitalist system from one angle or another. Barbès and Blanqui were fulminating against private property and preaching bloody revolution in *L'Homme Libre*; the Catholic priests Lamennais and Constant were putting forward their theories of Christian Socialism; Cabet had written a best-seller in his *Voyage to Icaria*, painting the most attractive of communist utopias; Pierre Leroux was preaching on the text of Equality and Louis Blanc had come down to brass tacks in his *Organization of Labour*; and Proudhon was becoming famous for his first memoir on property, published in 1840. Marx would have had no difficulty in coming into contact with any of these writers. He had taught himself to read, speak and write French, and he was soaking himself in their work and in a general study of French history culled especially from the Saint-Simonian historians, Thierry and Mignet.

The trouble was that he abominated the ideas of five of the eight Frenchmen who might have been most useful to the *Jahrbücher*, and two of the others abominated the *Jahrbücher*'s ideas. The preachers of bloody insurrection seemed childish to the philosopher in him; with Catholic priests, however unorthodox, he would have nothing to do; and as for Cabet, he had had enough of utopias since he had seen the damage that Robert Owen and Fourier had done in distracting effort from the transformation of society and diverting it into ludicrous little Harmonies and Phalansteries at the other side of the globe. Leroux and Louis Blanc might have had something really useful to say in the *Jahrbücher*, but they were deists, totally out of sympathy with the thinking of the German neo-Hegelians and particularly with that of Feuerbach. In fact the whole of French revolutionary thought in the first half of the nineteenth century was obsessed with Christianity or Deism. Only Proudhon might be an exception. As Marx wrote later: "At a time when the French Socialists prided themselves on their religious sentiments as something superior to the Voltairianism of the eighteenth century and to the German atheism of the nineteenth," Proudhon multiplied his attacks "against religion and against the Church."

Proudhon was out of Paris, away at Lyons working for the canal company, during Marx's first months in Paris. Marx could not meet him, and the first number of the *Deutsch-Französische Jahrbücher* went to press without any contribution from a French socialist. Everything in it was by a German or a German Jew, except for a letter from a Russian revolutionary, Bakunin. Marx's own chief contributions were essays on Hegelianism and on Judaism, in which he wrote of the proletariat and the Jews in identical terms. Both the proletarian and the Jew owed his position to the rôle that had been assigned to him by capitalist society. Each was "a sphere which cannot emancipate itself without emancipating all other spheres of society." It was clear from these essays that Marx had at last formulated the problem which he spent the rest of his life in trying to solve. It was also clear that he did not yet know what its terms meant. The "proletariat," for instance, was still an abstraction; he had no realization of what it actually was.

Marx's introduction to the proletariat came from Friedrich Engels, and his introduction to Engels came through the *Jahrbücher*. Engels submitted an article and came to Paris to discuss it with the editor. He stayed ten days with Marx in August 1844, and they began a relationship which became the most important thing in the lives of both of them. They had met eighteen months ago when Engels had called at the office of the *Rheinische Zeitung*, but the meeting had meant nothing to Marx. He saw a young man of twenty-two, blue-eyed and charming, full of dash and conversation and enthusiasm for the Saint-Simonian socialism which he had picked up from Moses Hess. Marx, in his suspicious way, thought that he had been sent as an emissary of Bauer and the Young Hegelians whom he was busy prising out of the columns of the *Zeitung*; he made the interview short and very cold. But in the Engels who came from Manchester to meet him in Paris, Marx saw a very different creature. Here was a man who had studied the new industrial system at its centre, a man who had got the facts about the proletariat—Engels had brought with him the materials for his book on *The Economic Condition of the Working Classes in England in 1844*. And here, what is more, was a disciple.

There could hardly be more sharply contrasting characters than those of Marx and Engels. Friedrich Engels was a light-hearted, warm-natured, life-loving man; Marx was morose, cold and interested neither in people, nature or art, except as the raw material for ideas. Engels had a marvellous facility for making friends, for love affairs, for learning languages, for writing anything from translations of Shelley and original poems to travel sketches, theatre criticism and social history. Marx had no such facilities—and for writing, especially when it came to writing anything to time or to a set length, he had a positive disability. Engels was of a natural modesty: he had recognized Marx as a genius and, as he was to write later, "genius is such an exceptional thing that we who have it not always know that we cannot attain it." Marx was unable to conceive what modesty or humility might mean. He was incapable of a relationship with a man who might compete with him. Engels was the first intelligent socialist he had met whose subservience he could take for granted.

Engels's experience was almost as valuable to Marx as his disposition. He came of a family of industrialists from Barmen-Elberfeld in the Wupperthal in Westphalia. His grandfather had founded a textile business, and had made a name for himself by being the first manufacturer to build houses for his workers. His father had developed the business by being the first Rhineland manufacturer to install

English machines and by opening a factory at Manchester. Friedrich Engels had not liked the prospect of going into the family firm; he had seen too much of industrialism in Elberfeld where the factory refuse poisoned the sweet river and the factory work poisoned not only the bodies but also the souls of the workers. They never sang, those workers, never danced; their only recreation was to get boozed in the gin-shops, and then, if the spirit moved them, to brawl. Friedrich Engels's father had the good sense to send him to learn the business from the Manchester end.

The Manchester of 1843–4 was a revelation to Engels, and through Engels it became a revelation to the rest of the world. He saw it sharply with his own eyes, and with those of an Irish girl, Mary Burns, one of his father's mill-hands, whom he made his mistress and set up with her sister in a house in Salford. Engels learned more of working-class conditions from Mary and Lizzie Burns than ever he could have seen for himself. If the picture was lighted with the fire of Irish indignation, it was none the worse for that; he had plenty of business colleagues to tone it down for him from the employers' point of view. From Engels, Marx learnt precisely and in human rather than statistical terms what was the condition of the working-class in England in 1844.

A few weeks after Engels went home to Barmen, Proudhon came to Paris. He remained there from September 1844 until after Marx left Paris in February 1845. This was the opportunity for the meeting to which Marx had been looking forward. France was the home of theoretical socialism, and Proudhon had been recognized since 1840 as the leading French socialist. Marx himself recognized him as such in the book which he was writing in the autumn of 1844, a book entitled *The Holy Family*, a polemic against Bruno Bauer and his brothers, which appeared in 1845 under the joint authorship of Marx and Engels, though Engels later denied that he had written more than a few pages of it. In a long chapter devoted to Proudhon, Marx wrote : "Proudhon submits private property, which is the basis of political economy, to a critical examination—to a serious examination, absolute as well as scientific. That is the great scientific progress that he has achieved, a progress which revolutionizes political economy and which presents, for the first time, the possibility of making political economy a true science. . . . Proudhon's work *What is Property?* has the same importance for economics as Siéyès's *What is the Third Estate?* has for politics. . . . Proudhon does not only write in the interest of the proletarians, he is a proletarian himself. His work is a serious manifesto of the French proletariat and has an historic importance altogether greater than that of the literary lucubration of an ordinary critic."

Of their meeting neither Marx nor Proudhon has left any considerable record. We know from Marx that they had "long discussions which sometimes went on all through the night." (And we know from other sources that Proudhon was well capable of discussing for twelve hours on end. A friend of his, getting tired of hearing him arguing with Bakunin about Hegel's system one evening in the musician Reichel's house, went away; when he came back to see Reichel next day, Proudhon and Bakunin were still sitting in the same place, still holding forth on Hegel.) Marx claimed : "I infected him, to his great detriment, with a Hegelianism which he could not go deeply into because he did not know German." It was quite true that Proudhon could not read German and he could not read Hegel's work in French because it had not yet been translated, but he had been infected with Hegelianism years before he met Marx. As early as 1839 he was writing to a friend : "Hegel's logic, such as I understand it to be, satisfied my reason infinitely more than all the old apothegms which have been stuffed into us from our childhood to account for the irregularities in our reasoning and in the community." Later he was re-infected with Hegelianism, but not so much by Marx as by one of Marx's *bêtes-noires*, Karl Grün. Marx's version of this was that "the work which I had begun was continued after my expulsion from France by Karl Grün, and this professor of German philosophy had the advantage over me in that he understood nothing of what he was teaching."

It would have been surprising if in their long discussions Marx had as much influence on Proudhon as Proudhon on Marx. The Frenchman was thirty-five years old, the German twenty-five; the former was already famous, the latter was still quite unknown. Proudhon had already studied the economists and had established himself as the first socialist to take the approach of economic science to what had hitherto been cloudy utopianism. This was a rôle which Marx had intended for himself. If he learned anything from Proudhon in 1844, he would have been the last man to admit it.

Before Marx's relationship with Proudhon went very far, he had to leave France. His relations with Ruge had deteriorated, as they were bound to do since the Marx family were living in his house. They quarrelled over money, and it must be admitted that Karl and Jenny had not learned to live cheaply.

Jenny's brother had sent Lenchen Delmuth, a peasant girl who had been a servant in the Westphalens' house, to look after Jenny who was pregnant. Arnold Ruge felt that they were setting up too grand an establishment. The *Deutsch-Französische Jahrbücher* could never have kept Marx, let alone his family; his main source of income during his time in Paris was a present of a thousand thaler from friends in Cologne. The *Jahrbücher* was a failure from the start, and it was obvious from the moment the first number appeared that there would never be another. It was of no interest to Frenchmen; the Prussian Government banned it, and their customs officials seized over 300 copies on the German frontiers. With the failure of the *Jahrbücher*, the Germans in Paris had no paper except the scurrilous little *Vorwärts*. This soon fell foul of the Prussian Court, which demanded its suppression. Guizot, the head of the French Government, was reluctant to take any notice of the demand, but he ended by issuing orders of expulsion against the refugees connected with the paper. Marx, who had already sent his family to Trier and who had just finished his book on *The Holy Family*, was in no mood to resist the order. On 1 February 1845 he left Paris for Brussels.

The months in Paris were the formative period of Marx's life. When he had left the Rhineland for Paris he could not in any sense be called a socialist; he was a philosopher with journalistic experience who was determined to apply philosophic analysis to the problems of contemporary society. When he left Paris for Brussels a year and a half later he was a dedicated socialist, and almost every one of the ideas which he spent the rest of his life in working out had already been formed in his mind. "I began my research into economics in Paris," he declared in the preface to *The Critique of Political Economy*; it was there that he first studied the English school of economists, particularly MacCulloch and Ricardo. He might have admitted, too, that he began his research into history at that time; for it was in Paris that he soaked himself in the history of France, notably in the social history of the fifty years since the great Revolution. It was there that he reached his Materialist Interpretation of History, the interpretation which sees economic factors as the causes of all historical change, the root from which all other changes, in thought and word and morals, stem. "When I met Marx, in Brussels, in the spring of 1845," wrote Engels, "he had already worked it out and laid it before me."

It was in Paris, too, that Marx first met working-class socialists and was introduced to what called itself a working-class movement. This consisted of an association known as the League of the Just, which Weitling, a Prussian tailor's apprentice, had founded to convert German workers abroad to socialism. Marx had attended meetings of this little group of a dozen German artisans in Vincennes. They were not proletarians in the sense of unskilled workers, and they were in no way typical of the new working-class which was being created by the development of machine industry in factories. His introduction to that new class he owed to the conversations and writings of Friedrich Engels. This second-hand knowledge he acquired in Paris, but he was to make a nodding acquaintance at first-hand in 1845. Engels joined Marx in Brussels, and persuaded him to accompany him on a journey to Manchester, where he wanted to see Mary Burns again and bring her back with him to the continent. Marx and Engels spent six weeks in England, and Marx had his first and almost his only sight of those sour fruits of the industrial revolution which put so much acid into his pen in later years. He saw Manchester at its worst, a sight which needs little imagination to turn into a revolutionary experience.

Not only did Marx become a convinced socialist; he also became convinced that he was the only true socialist. While he was in Paris he had written *The Holy Family* denouncing the Bauer brothers, and as soon as he had settled down in Brussels he turned to a denunciation of the other German socialists. There was a group which Karl Grün had had the impudence to call the True Socialists: this Marx anathematized in a vast book entitled *The German Ideology*. No publisher could be found for it, but the writing of it made him feel better. Now he undertook, with Engels and a certain Philippe Gigot, his first entry into practical politics. It was an attempt to begin the organization of international socialism by the innocent means of correspondence.

The project was outlined in a letter to Proudhon dated 5 May 1846. It is a strange letter, written by an unknown hand in passable French and signed Charles Marx. After preliminary courtesies Marx explains: "Jointly with my friends Friedrich Engels and Philippe Gigot (both in Brussels), I have organized with German communists and socialists a regular correspondence intended to be concerned both with the discussion of scientific questions and with the watch which must be kept on the popular press and on the socialist propaganda which may be made in Germany by those means. The principal aim of our correspondence will, however, be to put the German socialists in contact with the socialists of France and England, to keep the foreigners in touch with the socialist movements which will be in progress in Germany, and to inform the Germans in Germany of the progress of socialism in France and England. In this manner differences of opinion can be brought into the open; it will be possible to reach an exchange of ideas and impartial criticism. It will be a step that the Socialist Movement can take in *literary* expression to rid itself of the limitations of *Nationality*. And when the moment for action comes, it will certainly be of great importance for everyone to be conscious of the state of affairs abroad as well as in his own country." Marx goes on to invite Proudhon to undertake the Paris end of the correspondence.

It sounds a sensible request but, on the same page, sandwiched between Marx's letter and a polite note by Engels, is a postscript signed by Philippe Gigot which shows the cloven hoof : "I here denounce to you M. Grün, now in Paris. This man is nothing but a literary hack, a sort of charlatan who wants to make a living by exploiting modern ideas. He tries to hide his ignorance under pompous and arrogant phrases, but he does nothing but make himself ridiculous by his nonsense. This man is *dangerous*. He abuses the acquaintance he has made, by his impertinence, with celebrated authors so as to make a pedestal for himself and to compromise them with the German public. In his book on the French socialists he dares to call himself 'Proudhon's tutor'; he claims that he has revealed important axioms of German science to him. . . . Beware therefore of this parasite. Perhaps I shall have more to say to you later of this individual."

Proudhon's reply to this letter brings out in sharp

relief the contrast between the characters of the two great socialists. On the question of Karl Grün, Proudhon takes no notice of the fact that it has been raised by Gigot and writes direct to Marx: "I sincerely regret the little divisions which, it appears to me, exist in German socialism and of which your complaints against M. Grün give me the proof. I much fear that you have seen this writer in a false light, and I appeal, my dear Monsieur Marx, to your reconsideration. G. finds himself in exile, without any money but with a wife and two children and nothing to live on but his pen. What is there for him to make his living out of, if not by exploiting modern ideas? . . . Ah, if we were all millionaires, things would be different; we should all be saints and angels. But one must live, that is to say, buy bread and meat and fuel, pay for one's lodging; and, good heavens, the man who sells social ideas is not more unworthy than the man who sells a sermon." Proudhon goes on to say that he owes nothing to Grün as a tutor, but that he is in his debt for introducing to him and for translating for him "your writings, my dear Monsieur Marx, and those of M. Engels and the important works of Feuerbach"; and he adds that Grün has expressed the desire to translate Proudhon's new book into German, and that this would be of even more financial assistance to Grün than to the author if Marx would do what he can to promote its sale: "It would give me pleasure, my dear M. Marx, if you would withdraw the judgement [on Grün] which you made in a moment of irritation, for you were in a temper when you wrote to me."

This letter brings out the contrast between the approach to socialism of Marx and Proudhon even more sharply than that between their characters.

Proudhon takes up the phrase in Marx's letter about "the moment for action." "Perhaps," he writes, "you still hold the opinion that no reform is actually possible without a *coup de main*, without what used to be called a revolution but is really nothing but a shock. . . . I believe that we have no need of that for success, and that in consequence we ought not to put forward *revolutionary* action as the means of social reform, because this so-called means would simply be an appeal to force, an appeal to the arbitrary—in a word, a contradiction. The problem as I see it is this : *To bring back into society, by a new economic arrangement, the wealth that is being taken out of society by the present economic arrangements*. In other words, to turn the economists' theory against Property in such a way as not to endanger what your German socialists call *community* and what I confine myself for the moment to calling *liberty and equality*. Now, I think I know the means for solving, with no long delay, this problem; I prefer to burn Property over a slow fire rather than inflate it anew by having a St. Bartholomew Massacre of the property-owners. . . . I ought to say in passing that these seem to be the opinions also of the working-class in France : our proletarians have such a thirst for understanding that we would get a very bad reception from them if we gave them nothing to drink but blood. In a word, it would, in my opinion, be bad policy for us to speak as exterminators; the means of extreme action will easily be found; the people have no need of exhortation in that direction."

Proudhon went on to refuse Marx's invitation in words which expose the central difference between the two men : "Let us by all means collaborate in trying to discover the laws of society, the way in which these laws work out, the best method to set about investigating them; but, for God's sake, after we have demolished all the dogmatisms *a priori*, let us not of all things attempt in our turn to instil another kind of dogma into the people. Let us not fall into the contradiction of your compatriot Martin Luther, who, after overthrowing Catholic theology, addressed himself to the task of building up, with all the apparatus of excommunication and anathemas, a Protestant theology. For three whole centuries Germany has been doing nothing but pull down the plaster-work of Martin Luther. Let us not, by contriving any more such restrictions, leave any more such tasks for the human race. With all my heart I welcome your idea of exposing all opinions to the light. Let us have decent and sincere polemics; let us give the world an example of learned and farsighted tolerance. But simply because we are at the head of a movement, do not let us ourselves become the leaders of a new intolerance, let us not pose as the apostles of a new religion—even though this religion be the religion of logic, the religion of reason itself. Let us welcome, let us encourage all the protests; let us condemn all exclusions, all mysticisms. But never let us think of any question as closed, and even after we have exhausted our very last argument, let us begin again, if necessary, with eloquence and irony. On that condition I shall be delighted to associate with you—but otherwise, no!"

Thus was lost any opportunity there might have been for Marx and Proudhon to work together. The two main streams of socialist thought which might, had they flowed together, have led to the emancipation of the working-class, henceforth diverged. And there could be no question of Marx and Proudhon agreeing to differ. Henceforth they must fight, or rather Marx must fight Proudhon, for to Marx's mind whoever was not with him must be against him.

The occasion for attacking Proudhon in public arose before the year was out. In October 1846 Proudhon's first *magnum opus* was published by Guillaumin in Paris, two substantial volumes bearing the title *Système des Contradictions Economiques, ou Philosophie de la Misère*. The chief contradiction was the paradox, later to be so familiar, of poverty in the midst of potential plenty. Typically, Proudhon began the book with a dissertation on the idea of God. "The history of societies is for us nothing more than a long determination of the idea of God, a progressive realization of the destiny of Man." He went on to launch a double-edged attack on the bourgeois economists and the utopian socialists. "Two great forces are disputing the government of the world and anathematizing each other like two opposing canticles : Political Economy or tradition, Socialism or Utopia. . . . Political Economy tends to the consecration of egoism; Socialism leans towards the exaltation of the community . . . the Economists are optimists with regard to accomplished facts, the Socialists with regard to facts still to be accomplished." After a long analysis of competition and monopoly, of taxation and credit, of property and community, he ends with a magnificent chapter on population and the conclusion that "Destitution is always with us. Not for Malthus's reasons but because of a fault in the organization of work. After having provoked the consumption of goods by the abundance of products, society encourages a shortage by the low level of wages." The theory later to be called Under-Consumption emerges crystal-clear from Proudhon's *Philosophie de la Misère*.

Marx was furious with the book and wrote in French a savage onslaught on it, entitled *Misère de la Philosophie*, and containing what a recent critic has described as "the bitterest attack by one thinker on another since the celebrated polemics of the Renaissance." Marx declared that "Monsieur Proudhon flatters himself that he has criticized both economics and communism, but in reality he has remained far below either of them : below the economist because as a philosopher with a mystic formula in his pocket he imagines himself spared the necessity of going into economic details, and below the socialist because he has neither sufficient insight nor sufficient courage to raise himself, even speculatively, above the bourgeois horizon. He appears to be the synthesis, and in fact he is nothing but a composite error. He desires to hover above both bourgeois and proletarian as a man of Science, but in fact he is nothing but a petty-bourgeois thrown hither and thither between capital and labour, between economics and socialism. . . . What he trumpets into your ears with the voice of a blustering buffoon is his own glorification, wearisome nonsense and unending rhodomontade about his pretended 'science'."

Marx's book was published in Paris as well as in Brussels, but Proudhon refrained from publishing an answer. He contented himself with noting in the margin of his copy : "The real sense of Marx is that he regrets everywhere that my thought agrees with his and that I have expressed it before him. . . . The truth is that Marx is jealous." Which was indeed the truth.

Although the *Misère de la Philosophie* cut no ice at the time, when Marx's name was still unknown, it was by far the best thing that Marx had written so far, and except for the *Communist Manifesto* and *Capital* itself, nothing that he wrote later was either so readable or so important. It contains the nearest thing to a full statement that Marx ever published of that theory of the economic interpretation of history, or Historical Materialism, which was the basis of all his later work and which can be seen now as his main contribution not only to socialist ideology but to the general climate of thought in our own times. It makes him the father of modern historiography, if not of modern sociology as well; although the paternity may be disputed and the genes of the theory can be found in Proudhon and in earlier writers, the affiliation order must surely be made out to Marx. The motive force in history, he insisted, lies not in ideas, not in creeds, not in morals : it is to be found in the economic environment, in the tensions arising between the ruling class of possessors and the class which they exploit.

The theory was never more clearly expressed by Marx than in a letter to Annekov in about 1846 : "Are men free to choose this or that social form ? Not in the least. Take any particular stage in the development of the productive forces of man and you will find a corresponding form of trade and consumption. Take definite stages in the development of production, trade, consumption, and you have a corresponding form of social constitution, a definite organization of family, race or classes, in a word a corresponding form of civil society. Take such a civil society, and you have a definite political situation, which is only the official expression of civil society.

"It remains to add that men are not free masters of their forces of production—the foundation of their whole history—because these forces are acquired, are the product of previous activity. Thus the forces of production are the result of man's practical energy, but the energy is in itself conditioned by the circumstances in which men are placed by the forces of production already acquired by them, by the social forces existing before them, which they themselves have not created but are the product of the previous generation. In the simple fact that each generation finds itself confronted with forces of production acquired by the preceding one, which serves it as the raw material for new forces of production, it follows that there is a continuity in the history of mankind, and a history of mankind which is all the more his history because his forces of production and consequently his social relationships have grown in the meantime."

Elaborating the theory of Historical Materialism and excommunicating all heretics, from Grün to Proudhon, from the non-existent communion of communists, was not the only work of Marx in Brussels. He was reading omnivorously and struggling with insufficient means to bring up a young family in a wretched little house in a suburb (a daughter, Laura, was born in September 1845; a son, Edgar, in December 1846). He was writing more rapidly than at any other period of his life, both books and articles, notably in the *Deutsche Brüsseler Zeitung*, where he and Engels found particular enjoyment in laying about the Christians: "The social principles of Christianity justified slavery in the classical world and they glorified medieval serfdom, and if necessary they were quite willing to defend the oppression of the proletariat. . . . The social principles of Christianity preach the necessity of a ruling and an oppressed class, and all they have to offer to the latter is the pious wish that the former may be charitable."

But his main efforts in Brussels went into the attempt to build up an international socialist organization. He founded a little group of some seventeen members which he called the Communist Party, perhaps to distinguish it from the Socialist Party, founded by Louis Blanc. It was a group of writers, linked with Correspondence Committees in Germany and London and later in Paris, where Engels was to take the place which Proudhon had declined. There were no proletarians on these committees; they had to be sought in societies like the League of the Just and in the group of German exiles who had formed a German Workers' Educational Union in Brussels and in the international Fraternal Democrats who used to meet in the White Hart in Drury Lane. The idea was to co-ordinate all these organizations in a Communist League. Marx and Engels went to London at the end of November 1847 for a congress of the League at which they were assigned the task of writing a public manifesto describing the principles of communism—and therefore the purpose of the League. For some reason or another they seemed in no hurry to fulfil this assignment. Engels went back to Paris and Marx to Brussels, where he devoted himself to giving a course of lectures to a group of German exiles.

Meanwhile Proudhon was finding himself exhausted by the efforts which had gone into the writing of *La Philosophie de la Misère*. "It is the last book I shall ever write," he told his mother in a letter; "from now on I shall enter on another path."

He was not at all clear what this path would be. Even more than usual, money was lacking; his father had died in March, leaving him with his mother and his feckless brother Charles to support. The *Philosophie* seemed likely to bring him more notoriety than royalties. There might be more money in the technical works he had thrown off at the same period —one on Railways and Canals and another on the Organization of Credit—but he must still depend on the Gauthier job for anything in the way of a steady income.

Yet towards the end of 1847 Proudhon suddenly gave up his work with Gauthier and went to Paris. It seemed a foolish thing to do, for he had no close friends in the capital and no prospect of employment. Only 200 francs stood between him and starvation, and his project for founding a paper to be called *Le Peuple* was likely to lose more money than it gained. He said at the time that he went to Paris because he wanted to think and to pursue his studies in peace. In reality he went because he had a premonition of catastrophe and felt a need to be near the centre.

# Chapter Five

## 1848

THERE was a strange light over Europe in the winter of 1847–8. Still as the air before a snow-storm, there was an atmosphere of expectancy every-where, of waiting for something unpredictable, something that had never happened before. All over the continent—in Poland and Hungary, in Germany and Italy, in Spain and in France—a change of weather threatened, but what the change would mean, what direction it would come from, no one had any idea. Listening to the self-styled revolution-aries, reading their little journals and pamphlets, governments could excusably persuade themselves that nothing would happen. How could a political storm break if there was no indication of its direc-tion? Liberty, Equality, Fraternity were still catch-words everywhere, but what did they mean beyond vague aspirations, to be whipped like cream into a shapeless blob by an orator at a banquet, by an actor on a platform? Outside France, the revolutionaries wanted national independence, national unity; there at least was a policy, formulating a means if not an end. But in France, where nationalism was satisfied and civil liberties were comparatively secure, no one seemed to want anything tangible. Unless it were the vote. It would be a good thing to extend the franchise from property-owners to the people. But what the people could be expected to do with the vote was another question, never answered because never asked. Except by Proudhon, who concluded that "universal suffrage is the surest means for making the people lie."

The storm would be more than political—it would be social. What the inarticulate masses wanted was not the vote but the abolition of property rights. Only one Frenchman apart from Proudhon saw this. Alexis de Tocqueville, a Norman *grand seigneur*, fastidious and reserved, unbending and cold, presented a complete personal contrast to Proudhon, but he had started his life's work from the same principle—a love of liberty and equality and a realization of the difficult relationship between the two. In his great work on *Democracy in America*, de Tocqueville had forecast the dangers of democratic revolution, seeing how it might lead through demagogy to bureaucracy and centralization and to an increasingly inquisitorial State. "The revolutionaries," he wrote, "had sought to be free in order to make themselves equal; but in proportion as equality was more established by the aid of freedom, freedom itself remained more difficult of attainment." Proudhon had learned much from the author of *Democracy of America*, and his debt is reflected in his early works.

Perhaps de Tocqueville had learned from the author of *What is Property?* His prophetic speech in Parliament on 29 January 1848 had a Proudhonian echo: "As long as the right of property was the origin and groundwork of many other rights, it was easily defended—or rather it was not attacked; it was then the citadel of society while all the other rights were its outworks; it did not bear the brunt of attack and, indeed, there was no serious attempt to assail it. But today, when the right of property is regarded as the last undestroyed remnant of the aristocratic world, when it alone is left standing, the sole privilege in an equalized society, it is a different matter. Consider what is happening in the hearts of the working-classes, although I admit they are quiet as yet. It is true that they are less inflamed than formerly by political passions properly speaking; but do you not see that their passions, far from being political, have become social? Do you not see that, little by little, ideas and opinions are spreading amongst them which aim not merely at removing such and such laws, such a ministry or such a government, but at breaking up the very foundations of society itself?" They did not see; de Tocqueville talked in vain.

From his lodging on the Left Bank, Proudhon watched the storm coming. He described his mood of that winter in an article in *Le Peuple* a year later, none the less sincere for the grandiloquent tone which marked his first essays in journalism. Instead of welcoming the catastrophe he anticipated, as a revolutionary critic of society might have been expected to do, Proudhon dreaded it. "Placed at the very bottom of the social edifice, in the midst of the working masses, and being myself one of the sappers who had undermined the foundations, I could see, better than the statesmen who were arguing on the house-tops, the approach of danger and all the consequences of collapse. A few more days and, at the first parliamentary breeze, the Monarchy would crumble and with it the old structure of society. . . . The Houses of Parliament had not yet met for the 1847–8 session when I came to the conclusion that all was lost. I went straight to Paris. The two months that passed before the explosion—between the opening of the session and the fall of the throne—was the saddest, most wretched time that I have ever been through in all my life. The death of my mother, which happened in this interval, made only a slight impression on me at the time; even that was not enough to lift me out of my preoccupation. I understood then how much the claims of the mother-country are greater, for the citizen, than those of the family : Regulus and Brutus were explained to me. I trembled at the thought that no one I met believed in the coming of the Republic, or at any rate in such an immediate coming. . . . Before the birth of the Republic I was wearing mourning for it and expatiating on its sins."

By 22 February both Government and Republican Opposition in France had ceased to believe that any storm could break. The opposition cancelled the demonstrations which it had arranged for that day; the government withdrew its orders for military precautions. Both were taken by surprise when the people of Paris surged in hundreds of thousands into the streets. The masses did not know what they wanted. They came out on to the boulevards more out of curiosity than anything else, but once their mass-mood asserted itself they found that they wanted to get rid of King Louis-Philippe, rid of his Ministers, rid of the whole régime of moneyed men who had been getting rich at the expense of the workers. The following day the King dismissed his Prime Minister, Guizot, thinking to replace him by Thiers and that the ship of State would right itself by a slight change of course to the Left. But it was too late. The inevitable clash between troops and mob took place on the Boulevard des Capucines, and that night working-men were pulling up the pavements to build barricades and plundering the gunsmiths' shops for arms.

During the morning of 24 February the insurrectionaries gained control of the whole of the centre of the city, the troops not daring or not wishing to fire, until by ten o'clock only the Tuileries and the Palais Royal were held by the King's forces. At one o'clock Louis-Philippe abdicated, and for a few hours in the afternoon there were two governments in Paris—one representing the mob in the Hôtel de Ville, the other consisting of the constitutionally elected Opposition Members of Parliament. By evening the two had come together and the Second Republic was proclaimed, with an executive committee consisting of seven Deputies with the poet Lamartine at their head, three Left-wing members (Louis Blanc, Marrast and Flocon) and, for window-dressing, a worker called Albert. It was all over bar the shouting and the work.

The shouting has not yet died down; 24 February is still a symbol of glorious revolution in France. Hope swung higher that day than ever it was to rise again. As for the work—the achievement of social revolution and the rebuilding of society on the basis of justice—it was yet to come.

Proudhon was at the centre of the events of 24 February. He was not a man of action; he hated the process of insurrection as much as he distrusted the result; but the event swept him up willy-nilly, and it is fortunate for posterity that it did, for he left by far the best of all eye-witness accounts of the Revolution. Writing to his Besançon friend, Maurice, on the evening after the great day, he said: "Early in the morning, yesterday—Thursday—I set out on my campaign, beginning with a reconnaissance. More than five hundred barricades cluttering up the streets of Paris—a labyrinth of five hundred Thermopylaes. Towards midday, having seen everything, I went to the offices of the *Réforme*, in the Rue Jean-Jacques Rousseau, near to the central Post. The committee of Radicals, who the day before were asking for nothing more than the repeal of the September laws and a few other insignificant bits and pieces, who yesterday unanimously added to their programme electoral reform on a broad basis, who at noon were demanding in addition the Organization of Work and goodness knows what other platitudes, were talking by two o'clock of proclaiming the Republic. After the Chairman, Flocon, had fortified us with a quotation from Robespierre, like a captain who issues a ration of rum to his soldiers, I was given the job of going to a printer's to set up these fine words :

'Citizens : Louis-Philippe is assassinating you
as Charles X did.
Send him the way of Charles X !'

This was, I believe, the first Republican manifesto. 'Citizen,' old Flocon said to me as I was working at the printer's bench, 'you are holding a revolutionary fort; we count on your patriotism.' 'You can count on one thing,' I replied, laughing : 'I will not leave the job before I've finished it.' A quarter of an hour after the above proclamation was distributed, the shooting began at the Palais Royal, and soon the Tuileries were stormed. So much for the part that I played in the revolution."

The remarkable thing is that this day of action—when, among other things which he did not mention, the bespectacled philosopher helped to uproot trees in the Place de la Bourse and to lift paving-stones for the barricades—did not intoxicate Proudhon. He was eulogizing the Revolution at the instant of its outbreak, wearing mourning for it at the moment of its birth. In those cataclysmic days he was the only Frenchman, except de Tocqueville, who understood the deep significance of what was happening.

It is often said that the object of studying history is to discover what happened in the past, and it is said almost as often that the object is to disclose what is likely to happen in the future. Neither is the true object, though the discovery of the past is a necessary preliminary study and the disclosing of the future may be a useful by-product. The object of historical study is to enable one to understand what is happening now. It may sound easy, but it is the most difficult thing of all—as anyone will realize who has tried to study and to understand himself. It is comparatively simple to understand what happened to oneself in the past, and possible to see in broad outlines what tendencies and limitations will condition one's development in the future; but only the wisest man knows what is happening in him—what emotions are uppermost, what motives are operative—at the present moment. And that is the essential thing to know.

Proudhon understood the French Revolution of 1848, and understood it in the moment of its happening. The evidence is in his letters and his articles in *Le Peuple* and *Le Représentant du Peuple*. He never put his knowledge in final book-form, unless, disregarding the title, we give the name of history-book to his *Confessions d'un Révolutionnaire pour servir à l'histoire de la Revolution de février*, written all three hundred pages of it, in six weeks in 1849. But the kernel of historical wisdom is there, the wisdom which sees the present moment in its essential relation to the past and to the future.

If Proudhon had been left alone to think, the world might have had an important addition to its shelf of historical classics. The author of *What is Property?* did not deserve to be left in peace, however dearly he desired it. In the evening of 26 February, when he was in the middle of another letter to Maurice, four workers, led by his admirer Duchêne, burst into his room. A postscript was added to the letter: "Four citizens, armed with muskets, have just this minute left my room. They came to ask me when I reckon to publish the volume which I have been promising for the last year. As I have often said to you, the Revolution has no idea behind it. . . . If I could write like M. Lamartine, I'd be the first man in France within a month."

The four armed men, compositors all, offered to provide paper and a printer for the journal which Proudhon had wanted to edit—*Le Représentant du Peuple*. Almost overnight the philosopher found himself a publicist, in duty bound to pass judgement on the events of the day without time for reflection; the student found himself an organizer of economic revolution, expected to find constructive solutions for problems which he was still in the process of analysing. But at the age of thirty-nine Proudhon had been a student too long, and as a philosopher he had been overfond of polemics. Since he must needs take part in the Revolution, it was better that his rôle should be at the desk than on the platform or the barricade. And so the publicist's work began in earnest. Parisians saw nothing of Proudhon throughout the spring, but they began to talk of him, for if the articles in the *Représentant* could be ignored, the three pamphlets that appeared between March and June could not. They were entitled *Solution du Problème Sociale, Organization du Crédit* and *Résumé de la Question Sociale*.

The Revolution had no idea behind it. Parliamentary government based on manhood suffrage offered no solution to the economic problem. The masses wanted more than the vote; they wanted food and work. Unemployment figures rose from 8,000 in March to 50,000 in April; by June they would reach 100,000. "The right to work" was the slogan of the masses, and now that its author, Louis Blanc, was Minister of Labour, there was no excuse for postponement. From every quarter of France the beggars were coming to town, making their way to Paris to demand the fulfilment of promises which the new Ministers had given so glibly in their opposition days. The Ministers found themselves on the horns of a dilemma which no liberal revolutionaries have ever escaped : they must either impose reforms by dictatorial methods and so cease to be liberals, or they must proceed as liberals and adjourn the revolutionary reforms. It is small wonder that Lamartine and his colleagues should have sought refuge behind a smoke-screen of rhetoric from which nothing concrete emerged except National Workshops. This last was a very old expedient. Public works had been used by every government since Louis XIV in time of crisis. As a temporary measure, they may succeed well enough : setting men to dig holes in the ground and fill them up again, in return for a living wage, is better than idleness and starvation. But as a lasting reform, as a method of *l'Organization du travail*, National Workshops would be worse than useless.

And a lasting reform was what the masses in 1848 expected them to be.

The Provisional Government was riding for a fall, and Proudhon's immediate task was to prevent the disaster. In place of rhetoric and slogans, the Republic must be given an idea and a programme. Proudhon's teaching, in articles and pamphlets, was simple and concrete. The Revolution, he insisted, must be economic as well as political. The economic necessity was not to organize the Right to Work, which could lead to nothing but loss of liberty and of wealth. National Workshops, as he had pointed out long ago in a letter to the Besançon Academy in January 1841, were an absurdity. "They will open during a slump. But slumps come through lack of markets, and how can national workshops find markets when private shops cannot? How can this competition ever end the crisis? And Government will need capital to pay the workers, capital from taxes, taxes from industry. Thus private industry will be supporting at its own cost an invincible competitor."

The necessity, Proudhon insisted, was to organize the Right to Credit. Every piece of useful work constituted a value; let every product be valued in a cheque drawable on a Credit Bank, and let these cheques be accepted as currency; the outcome would be the free circulation of goods, the increase of demand and the abolition of unemployment. Proudhon drew up a detailed scheme for a People's Credit Bank and sent it to Louis Blanc, but the Minister was too busy to give it proper consideration.

On the political side the Republic had nothing to offer beyond manhood suffrage. Proudhon had always seen the weakness of this, and the famous General Elections of April, when five million peasants cast votes for the first time, turned out to be confirmation of his warning. They returned a Conservative National Assembly containing more landed gentry and more Catholic partisans than any Assembly under the monarchy of Louis-Philippe. Proudhon's main case against Parliamentary Government was that it could solve nothing and that the democrats who supported it must inevitably be led towards centralization, authoritarianism and State Socialism, which were the direct negation of the liberty that they had desired to support. Proudhon insisted on decentralization, anarchism and the necessity of social rather than State action. Revolution could not be made by decrees : it might be made by men deciding to rely on themselves.

Proudhon's position as a publicist made it inevitable that he should be called to Parliament. He was nominated in five constituencies for the April Elections, and it was impossible for the editor of *Le Représentant du Peuple* to refuse to be the representative of the people. His election-address to the voters of the Doubs division indicated that he had neither taste nor talent for parliamentary work : "Dear fellow-countrymen, I need not add that I desire the fulfilment of the February Revolution : that means the Republic : that means more liberty for everyone, more equality, more well-being and less chatter and above all less governmental *bon plaisir*. That is enough to show you how little store I set on a debater's services and how I repudiate the intervention of the State in the Organization of Work." Proudhon was not returned at the General Election, but at a by-election in Paris on 4 June, 77,000 votes sent him to the National Assembly. Here with his usual conscientiousness he worked like a galley-slave, sitting through endless debates, pulling his weight on committees, driving his own oar through the choppy water of the Finance Commission, and in so doing lost contact with the subtle currents of public opinion, a contact which, as he knew, constituted his one qualification to represent the people. "Elected a fortnight ago as representative of the people, I entered the National Assembly with the timidity of a child and the ardour of a neophyte. From nine in the morning I was assiduous in attendance at meetings of committees and commissions, and I did not leave the House until evening, worn out with fatigue and disgust. . . . I knew nothing, either of the situation in the National Workshops, nor of the Government's policy, nor of the intrigues with which the Assembly was riddled. . . . And to realize how the people who are most completely ignorant of the condition of a country are nearly always those who represent it, one must have lived in that isolation which is called a House of Parliament. . . . They never spoke of the National Workshops except with a sort of terror : fear of the people is the disease of all who are in authority. For the Government, the people is the enemy. Every day we voted new subsidies to the National Workshops, while trembling at the incapacity of the Government and at our own impotence."

This fortnight in June was crucial for the Second Republic. Popular patience was near breaking-point as midsummer came without a single blossom on the tree of liberty planted so blissfully in February. An ill-timed announcement that the Workshops would be closed brought the mob out into the streets of Paris shouting "Bread or lead, bullets or work," and when neither bread nor work was forthcoming barricades were raised in the working-class quarters. The insurrection had neither programme nor leaders, but it had arms in its teeth and the wolf of famine at its back. The National Assembly, in a panic, vested all executive powers in the Minister of War, General Cavaignac, who with a soldier's simplicity set 40,000 regular troops and national guards to storm the barricades in the St. Antoine and Temple districts. For four days—from 22 to 26 June— civil war raged, and in the end a thousand corpses were lying on the hot pavements of Paris and five thousand prisoners were awaiting transportation. The Assembly voted by a large majority that Cavaignac had "deserved well of his country" and should continue to wield the executive power. "The memory of the June Days," wrote Proudhon, "will weigh for ever on my conscience. I confess with remorse that until the 25th I foresaw nothing, knew nothing, understood nothing."

Proudhon realized that the Revolution had foundered, but there was much that could be saved from the wreck. The leaders of the Provisional Government, Lamartine and Ledru-Rollin, were discredited by their ineffectiveness; Cavaignac would soon be discredited by his repressive measures; the Assembly was reactionary and impotent; but Government of some sort there must be, and the task was to take the essential business of organizing credit out of its hands. He pressed on with his proposal of a People's Bank, which now took the form of a society which would provide credit to its members without charging interest. More immediately there was the need to revive trade. The means to this end, Proudhon insisted, were to reduce taxes, prices and debts, and to accelerate by all means the velocity of circulation of money. He tabled a motion in the Assembly proposing that all landlords, houseowners, shareholders and creditors should sacrifice a third of the sum due to them in rent and interest, half of this money to go to the State and half to remain in the hands of the debtors.

A month ago Proudhon might have had a favourable hearing in the Assembly, but now the Deputies had a crying need to blame somebody for the June Days, and Proudhon was the most convenient scapegoat. He had no party behind him and belonged to no club. It was easy to make out that the author of the slogan *Property is Theft* was an irresponsible agitator, easy to quote passages from his articles in the *Représentant du Peuple* to prove that he condoned the worst excesses of the June insurrectionaries. "The German workman does not blush to beg his bread from workshop to workshop; the Spanish *lazarillo* goes further, he demands charity at the point of his dagger; the French worker asks for work, but you offer him alms and he rises, he fires his gun at you. I prefer the French workers, and I glory in belonging to this proud race." It would have been possible, of course, to quote passages from that same article of 5 July to prove that Proudhon deplored the rising ("We must recognize that the civil war which has spattered the cradle of the Republic with blood is an appalling misfortune, but that—thanks to Heaven—there are no guilty men, there are only victims"); possible to show that Proudhon, so far from being an advocate of class-war, had been a preacher of conciliation ("Workers, hold out your hand to your employers and, employers, do not repudiate the advances of those who were your workmen!"—Proudhon's electoral address to the Doubs voters in April); but that did not suit the book of the Assembly. Cavaignac suspended the *Représentant* and the Deputies got ready to haul down the wild man who had dared to table his subversive motion.

Proudhon was no orator. We shall never know whether he had it in him to become one. His address to the Assembly on 31 July was the first public speech he had ever made (unless we count the defence he read at Besançon assizes), and it was almost his last. He had no practice in public speaking and no taste for it. The address he now read to the Assembly was confused, halting, passionate and largely inaudible. Thanks to the constant interruptions by the gently nurtured Deputies—they were mostly landed gentry, bankers, prelates and generals, who punctuated the maiden speech with cries of "To the Zoo with him!" and "Down with the coward!"—Proudhon was on his feet for more than three hours. Thiers, replying, had no difficulty in making the peasant's son look foolish. He proposed that "considering that Citizen Proudhon's motion is an odious attack on the principles of public morality, that it violates the principle of property, that it encourages deflation, that it appeals to the basest passions; and considering also that the orator has calumniated the Revolution of February in pretending that it was associated with the theories he has described—the National Assembly passes on to the next business." Thiers's proposition was carried by 681 votes to 2. Only one Deputy voted with Proudhon, the weaver Greppo, a friend from his Lyons days.

Outside the Assembly the repercussion of these proceedings was enough to make Proudhon the hero of the hour with the masses. Financial backing was forthcoming to launch a new paper, *Le Peuple*, which reached a freak circulation of 70,000 copies.

Proudhon was now, in his eccentric way, a man to be reckoned with. Louis Bonaparte, who had been returned to the National Assembly at a by-election at the same time as Proudhon, was anxious to sound him on the question of the Presidency of the Republic. The new Constitution was in the making, and a majority in the Assembly had come round to the idea that there should be a single elected House as the legislative power, with a President, elected directly by the people, as head of the executive. Louis Bonaparte saw his opportunity. He had a past to live down —the foolish conspiracy which he had led in Strasbourg in 1836, the equally foolish landing at Boulogne in 1840 which had earned imprisonment under the monarchy of Louis-Philippe. But his name would not be against him with the peasants: they always remembered that it was his uncle who had assured them ownership of their land. He might not be unacceptable to the Left : had he not written some socialist books during his captivity in the castle of Ham? Might not Proudhon and his associates be the first to welcome a man who had the interests of the peasants closely at heart, who was distrusted by the financiers and the clericals, and who had proclaimed himself a socialist outside the socialist orthodoxy? The Prince asked Proudhon to come and see him. Proudhon was surprised and suspicious—an interview with a Bonaparte would not be without its compromising side—but his suspicions were overcome when he remembered that Louis Blanc had visited the Prince in London and that Ledru-Rollin knew about the present invitation. In any case, Proudhon would not be going alone: two other Deputies, Schmeltz and Joly, would be with him.

The interview with Louis Bonaparte took place on 20 September. That night Proudhon wrote in his diary: "Visit to Louis Bonaparte. The man seemed well-meaning—a chivalrous head and heart, more full of his uncle's glory than of personal ambition. On the whole, a mediocre intelligence. I doubt whether, on a close view and intimate acquaintance, he will amount to much. Still, I must *be on my guard*. It's the habit of every candidate to make up to the party leaders first."

Proudhon remained on his guard. His colleagues in the Assembly did not. They voted the new Constitution in November, including the provision that a President of the Republic should be elected immediately by direct vote of the people. Unlike his colleagues, Proudhon knew what this would mean. It would mean Louis Napoleon; and Louis Napoleon would mean the Emperor Napoleon. In a long article in *Le Peuple,* impressive for its sustained sarcasm and invective, Proudhon described why the masses would vote for Napoleon and what their choice would involve. "Come then, Napoleon, come and take possession of this race of Tartufes, of this people of courtesans. They say that you are only a half-wit, an adventurer, a fool. You have joined the police and played the fool in your time: you have all the makings of a Nero, of a Caligula—except their ferocity, which is no longer in fashion. Come, I tell you, you are the man that we need. Come and bring these bourgeois to reason; come and take their last child, their last shilling. Come and take vengeance on Socialism, Communism, Fourierism and all. Come now: the apostates of every régime are wait-

ing, ready to lay down their consciences and their
wives for you! Your uncle Jérôme once said, in his
petition to Louis-Philippe, that he only asked, on his
return to France, to be allowed to live and die as a
French citizen. But you, you know better: your
family has greater things in store for it. One glory
was still lacking to the name of Bonaparte. Come
then, put an end to our discords by taking our liberties! Come and consummate the shame of the
French people! Come, come, come! . . ."

On 10 December the presidential plebiscite was
held and Louis Bonaparte was elected by five million
votes, against two million for Cavaignac and a mere
twenty thousand for Lamartine. The new President
solemnly took the oath, "In the presence of God and
before all men, to be faithful to the democratic Republic and to defend the Constitution." Proudhon,
who had been wise before the event, was not prudent
after it. "Bonaparte, elected by the reactionaries, instrument of the reactionaries, personification of reaction," he wrote in *Le Peuple* on 25 January 1849,
"Bonaparte is at this moment the whole of the reaction, to such a point that whoever opposes Bonaparte is really revolutionary, and if Bonaparte were
to fall, the whole conspiracy of doctrinaires, legitimists, Orléanists, Imperialists, Capitalists and Jesuits
would crumble away with him! . . . The election of
10 December, you must never forget, was sprung on
the nation; I almost said it was an outrage on the
national reason."

For his attacks on the President, the Assembly repealed the immunity from arrest which Proudhon
enjoyed as a Deputy. On 28 March 1849 he was
brought before the Seine Assizes on a charge of sub-

versive activities and sentenced to a fine of ten thousand francs and three years' imprisonment.

When 1848 began, Marx was writing and seeing through the press the manifesto commissioned by the Communist League. The *Communist Manifesto* was published in Germany in February, too late to have an effect on the events of the year, but early enough to get Marx into trouble with the Brussels police, who arrested him and Jenny and ordered their expulsion from Belgium. This was the day before the Paris revolution of 24 February. Marx got a letter from Flocon inviting him to come and play a part in the revolution.

Back in Paris, Marx set up a new headquarters of the Communist League and plunged into insurrectionary politics. But his plunge was not in an extremist direction. The German exiles were all agog for an "invasion" of Germany: they wanted to form an "army" and to march across the frontiers to fight for the liberation of their brethren. Marx did his best to restrain them. He knew that all talk of invasion and armies was romantic fantasy, and that the only way for socialists abroad to make themselves useful in Germany was for them to set about propagandist and organizing work. For he saw that the situation in Germany and the rest of Central Europe was very different from that in France. In Paris, where there had been a more or less bourgeois government since 1830, there might be a chance of a socialist victory. In the German and the Central European States it was the bourgeoisie which was rising against what might be called feudalism: the rôle of socialists at this stage would be to combine with the more radical bourgeois forces; they were too weak to do anything effective by themselves.

When the news reached Paris of the revolutions of 13 March in Vienna and of 18 March in Berlin, Engels went back to Wupperthal and Marx to Cologne. Here he managed to persuade some liberal industrialists to put up money to found a new *Rheinische Zeitung*, which he turned into a propagandist paper for democracy. He kept its columns clear of all talk of communism and directed the paper towards agitation for a united Germany on a radical but not a working-class basis. This outraged all his communist colleagues, whose Communist League he dissolved in spite of their protests and whose friends in Magyar and Slav countries he attacked in his leading articles. Marx had no use for nationalism except in so far as it might lead to the overthrow of the ruling class. Pan-German nationalism might possibly succeed in doing that, but nationalist risings in Hungary and the Slav countries would have the opposite effect : they would do nothing but replace German rule by that of native grandees.

After a few months the *Rheinische Zeitung* took its place as the most hard-hitting paper in Germany. It advocated war against Russia—always a popular note to strike for German ears. It urged a German war against Denmark for the seizure of Schleswig-Holstein, and this was even more popular. It attacked the Frankfurt Parliament for dithering and for burying itself in philosophical debates when it should have been taking action. It tried to goad the successive liberal governments of Prussia into making a reality of their position of power.

In all this, of course, it was to fail. There was no war against the Czar, who would survive to tighten his reign of terror in Poland; the war for Schleswig-Holstein was abandoned by the Prussian King, who did not even consult the National Assembly when he made a truce with Denmark; the Assembly itself collapsed under the weight of its own constitutional documents; and the liberal governments of Prussia gave way to the King and his reactionary party. But failure or no failure, it would be hard not to admit that Marx had been right in his propaganda policy. From the point of view of establishing socialism in Germany, his line was the correct though not the direct one.

Yet this policy of an alliance between socialists and liberals—of urging liberals to lead a revolution for the people—irked him, and he could not resist writing straight from the heart in the *Rheinische Zeitung* about the June Days in Paris: "The fraternity of the two opposing classes (one of which exploits the other) which in February was inscribed in huge letters upon all the façades of Paris, upon all the prisons and all the barracks . . . this fraternity lasted just so long as the interests of the bourgeoisie could fraternize with the interests of the proletariat. Pedants of the old revolutionary tradition of 1793, socialist systematizers who begged the bourgeoisie to grant favours to the people, and were allowed to preach long sermons . . . needed to lull the proletarian lion to sleep; republicans who wanted the whole of the old bourgeois system, minus the crowned figurehead, legitimists who did not wish to doff their livery but merely to change its cut—these had been the people's allies in the February revolution! Yet what the people hated was not Louis-Philippe but the crowned domination of a class, capital enthroned."

This was enough to alarm the capitalists who were

financing the *Rheinische Zeitung*. They began to withdraw their support, and a money-raising tour which took Marx as far afield as Austria in August was not successful. The German revolution had ceased to revolve. The end came on 1 November when the Austrian Government, having surrounded Vienna with 60,000 troops, crushed the workers' movement after a three-day struggle. Marx was now losing his bearings. He seemed to think that the French proletariat could rise and lead the workers of Europe in a war against Britain, which had taken Russia's place in his mind as the arch enemy. In his article in the *Rheinische Zeitung* in the last day of 1848 he insisted that "war against Britain is necessary because Britain has taken her place at the side of the counter-revolutionary forces, because Britain's interest is to defend the monopoly of capitalism and her policy is to uphold the existing social order; because, not content with holding down her own proletariat, she loves to enrol the German, French and Italian bourgeoisie, and because any social upheaval in France will be checked by the British bourgeoisie in their determination to defend their own interests, and because the old régime in Britain can be broken only by a world war which will provide the Chartists with the opportunity for a rising against their monstrous oppressors."

With the editor in this mood, the *Rheinische Zeitung* was not likely to survive for very long. All the funds that Marx could raise from his father's estate —he even pawned the family silver—would not have been enough to keep the paper afloat had not the Government provided its editor with a piece of unexpected publicity. The Prussian Government ordered the dissolution of the Assembly, and the As-

sembly retaliated by declaring all taxes imposed by
the Government to be illegal. Marx took up this
declaration and urged his readers to pay no taxes.
He was put on trial for incitement to sedition, and
the Cologne jury, after listening to a long harangue
from the accused, thanked him for his lecture and
acquitted him. The circulation of the *Rheinische
Zeitung* thereupon rose to 6,000; it was a time when
no English paper except *The Times* was selling more
than 8,000.

Karl Marx was now, at the age of thirty, in the
prime of life. A young man called Schurz who was
later to be an American senator has left a picture of
him : "A thick-set man with his broad forehead and
dark flashing eyes, his jet-black hair and full beard,
immediately attracted general attention. He had the
reputation of being a very considerable scholar in his
own field and, in fact, what he said was weighty,
logical and clear, but never have I met a man of
such offensive, insupportable arrogance. No opinion
which differed essentially from his own was accorded
the honour of even a half-way respectful consideration. He answered all arguments which displeased
him with a biting scorn for the pitiable ignorance of
those who advanced them, or with a libellous ques-
tioning of their motives. I still remember the cutting,
scornful tone with which he uttered—I might almost
say 'spat'—the word *bourgeois*; and he denounced
as 'bourgeois'—that is to say, as an unmistakable
example of the lowest moral and spiritual stagnation
—everyone who dared to oppose his opinions."

The Prussian Government, foiled by the court's
acquittal but understandably determined to get rid
of Marx, remembered that he had, while in Brussels,
given up his Prussian citizenship and was therefore

liable to expulsion as a foreigner. To this expulsion order there could be no answer. Marx went to Paris in July 1849, to the miserable post-revolutionary Paris where every socialist and most radicals were already in prison or in hiding. The French Government served him with an order restricting his residence in France to the district of Morbihan in Brittany. Marx preferred to leave France altogether. Waiting only till a subscription to meet his travelling expenses had been raised by his friends, he went in August 1849 to London where he was to stay for the rest of his life.

*Chapter Six*

# The Doldrums

THE failure of the 1848 revolutions meant that there was no longer any question of a working-class movement, let alone of a socialist movement. The revolutions had on the whole been middle-class affairs, but the hopes of socialists had depended on them; after their failure there could be no more hope. The old ruling classes were back in control of every country in Europe. Socialism was in the doldrums, and in the doldrums it must remain for a decade or more. When at last the wind came back into its sails, it came with the inspiration of Proudhon and of Marx, who almost alone among socialists of their generation had kept their minds ventilated during the years of stagnation.

Although he had been sentenced to a three-year term in March 1849, there was no need for Proudhon to go to prison. The court had in effect asked him "to go away and sin no more; and if that effort be too great, to go away at any rate." The condemned man had no difficulty in leaving Paris. He stayed at Lille for a while and then crossed the frontier to Brussels, but he did not take kindly to exile and in a few weeks he was back in Paris, lodging under an assumed name in the Rue de Chabrol. He took no precautions beyond the assumed name, attempted no disguise, and it was in broad daylight

95

that the police saw him, wearing his familiar spectacles and printer's blouse, taking a constitutional near the Gare du Nord. They arrested him and took him to the Sainte-Pélagie prison to serve his sentence.

Proudhon was delighted with his imprisonment. It gave him a rest, which he had been wanting for a long time. In December 1848, writing to Antoine Gauthier about a duel in which he had found himself engaged with the socialist, Félix Pyat, he had said: "It was a great stupidity of mine to fight that duel. . . . We blazed at each other, Pyat and I, like two beasts, at twenty yards' range. I should have liked to get a bullet in the thigh, so as to have six weeks' rest." Prison gave him more than rest, and more than those desiderata of philosophers—regular meals and free lodging; it gave him time to work and opportunity to regain his sense of perspective.

Sainte-Pélagie was certainly the mildest of all prisons. Situated in a quiet quarter of Paris and built as a *pension* for erring girls, its atmosphere was more that of a family hôtel than of a gaol. The political prisoners inhabited a separate building, known as the Pavilion; they were allowed to receive visitors and even to go out, so long as they behaved well and promised to return before midnight. "Here in Ste. Pélagie," he wrote to his friend Maurice in October 1849, "I am as well off as one can possibly be in prison. I have a room about five metres each way, with two windows looking out on the Pitié and the Jardin des Plantes. Even in the rue Mazarin when I was a Deputy, I was not so well lodged. I eat the prison bread, which is good; I take the midday soup, with meat twice a week and without on the other five days, and anything else I want I can get sent in from the restaurant. The authorities provide a wine at twelve sous a litre which is better than the wine merchants would sell at one franc fifty. I receive my visitors in my own room, and I have obtained permission to have newspapers and pamphlets. I've had all my old books sent—in fact, everything I possess is locked up with me. My desire is, in spite of the annoyance of prison and the physical and moral inconvenience which goes with it, to remain where I am for at least eighteen months."

In fact Proudhon enjoyed the last six months of 1849 more than any other period of his life. With the financial support of Herzen, whom he had met in Bakunin's rooms in 1847, he founded a new paper, *La Voix du Peuple*, to take the place of *Le Peuple* which had been condemned. He held editorial conferences in his prison cell, and drove his colleagues in the office to distraction by sending orders and articles which would be enough to get them all consigned to less commodious gaols. He dashed off the *Confessions d'un Revolutionnaire* with an ease and vigour which he had never equalled before. The *Confessions* were published in November, and in December Proudhon, on leave from his prison cell, got married.

The bride was a Parisian girl of twenty-six, by name Euphrasie Piégard, by profession a lace-maker. Though it came as a surprise to his friends, who had thought of Proudhon as a confirmed bachelor, there was nothing precipitate about the match. He had met the girl and proposed to her in February 1847. The real reason why he had come back from Brussels in the spring of 1849, the reason why he had taken to promenading the streets of Paris in broad daylight under the noses of the police, was that he was courting and did not intend there to be anything hole-and-corner about his courtship. "The presence of a

woman in my home has become necessary to me,"
he wrote in a letter of the time; "without that I
should become a savage. I came back to Paris to see
if I could realize a project which I had been cherish-
ing for two years." Mademoiselle Piégard was fourteen years younger than Proudhon. One of his
friends remembered having met her one day, coming
out of Proudhon's lodging—a fair-haired girl de-
cently escorted by her mother. They were working-
class people, a family of the same sort as Proudhon's
own.

His bride took a room in the rue de la Fontaine,
which Proudhon could see from his window in
Sainte-Pélagie, and was even allowed to visit occasionally. She followed him through the vicissitudes
of 1850, when he was hauled before the court on a
charge concerning *La Voix du Peuple* in January,
involved in more trouble over the newspaper in
February which got him removed to the Conciergerie, in trouble over a further seditious article in
April and removed to the citadel of Doullens. In
May he was back again in the Conciergerie, un-
abashed and starting a new weekly newspaper, *Le
Peuple*, which appeared regularly from June to
October. She gave birth to a daughter in November,
a child whom they called Catherine, after Proudhon's mother—"a name which caused a lot of
amusement; the name of Catherine is quite out of
fashion." She was pregnant again when Proudhon
was moved back to his old cell in Sainte-Pélagie in
the autumn of 1851, under a lighter régime which
allowed him to dine in her room and gave him three
days' leave every month. The following January the
second child was born—Marcelle. There were to be
two more, born when the father was no longer a

prisoner and there was a home of sorts for the young family.

Though Proudhon was inconceivably happy, he found it necessary when writing to his literary friends to make excuses for his marriage with an entirely un-intellectual woman. "I did not think it permissible to refuse her devotion after having aroused her af-fections," he wrote to Ackermann in October 1851. "It is the best thing—the most valuable to me and the most honourable in my own eyes—that I have done in my life. I made this marriage with premedi-tation, without passion, so as to be in my turn the father of a family, to live my life wholly, and to have by me, amid the storms into which I am launched, the image of maternal simplicity and modesty. My wife might well be more learned without my finding it at all objectionable; but that is not her fault or mine. Work and suffering have given her instead a fund of common sense which has its value." And in March 1854, writing to Bergmann after a lapse of seven years: "I married at the age of forty a young and poor working-woman, not for passion—you know where my passions lie—but out of sympathy for her position, respect for her person, and because, my mother having died, I had no family, because— will you believe it?—in default of love I had a mind for a home, for paternity. I had no other thoughts. In the last four years my wife has given me three little girls, pink and fair, whom their mother has nursed herself and whose existence fills almost all my spirit. It might be said that I should have conducted myself with more prudence, that it is not enough that children be brought into the world but they must be educated and provided with dowries. What is cer-tain is that paternity has filled a great void in me:

that it has given me a ballast that I lacked before and a drive such as I have never known."

There was no doubt about the drive. In July 1851 the prisoner published *l'Idée Générale de la Révolution au XIX<sup>e</sup> Siècle*, the book which contained the first full statements of the ideas of Anarchism and Federalism, ideas which would stand as his chief contribution to political science. The thesis was that the Revolution, a continuous process in which the 1789 constitution was the first modern milestone, had lost its direction when it concentrated on reforming the political hierarchy. Political powers always tend towards centralization, and thence towards tyranny. All concentration should be on the organization of economic forces. The true idea of the Revolution is to base society on economic forces organized without coercion by Government. The watch-words are Liberty and Justice; the principle is "Do as you would be done by"; the fundamental law is the law of contract.

Coming down to brass tacks, Proudhon insists that the first task is to get rid of the seigneurial rights of capital. This must be done by setting up a National Bank, independent of the Government, which will reduce interest rates. The National Debt, or rather the Government's debt to its citizen-creditors, will be paid off in successive conversions, the interest payments being deducted from the principal. Similarly, tenants and farmers and creditors of private concerns will have a right to property in their houses and holdings proportionate to the rent they have paid or the interest received. When the strangle-hold of Capital has thus been loosened, the way will be clear for the organization of commercial and industrial undertakings by the producers themselves. The small independent artisan and trader will have a free hand. In big concerns the associated workers, bourgeois and proletarian, will form a Syndicate for management and control. These Syndicates and the associations of little men will be the basis of the new society. Government will gradually be reduced to the rôle of a statistical bureau. The people will police themselves, set up their own courts of arbitration, their own social services. Anarchism, or non-Government, will be within sight. As for foreign affairs, they will be conducted between neighbour nations of Syndicalists and Anarchists, for France's neighbours will follow the same course as France, and a federation of free states will be the outcome.

A Utopian book certainly. But Proudhon might well ask whether his ideas were any more hopelessly Utopian than the ideas of 1848 had proved to be. Nearly all the leaders of the February Revolution were in exile or prison. Proudhon saw a whole menagerie of them at Doullens in 1850—Blanqui, Barbès, Raspail, Considérant, Louis Blanc, Ledru-Rollin and others—and made some nice observations on the nature of democratic leaders. "I should like to show you all these men," he wrote to his Polish friend, Charles Edmond. "One a well-meaning fanatic; the second a demagogic orator and vulgar careerist; the third, a mentally sick man, his brain a little cracked (he belongs to the most numerous category); the fourth playing the good fellow but having the wits of a fox underneath; and then, keeping close to the more or less gallant and clever leader, the grasping and cruel lieutenant—the jackal following the lion. A portrait gallery of them would destroy the demagogic party in twenty-four hours, though in the present state of things that would be playing into the hands of the reactionaries."

The Liberals were doing no better than the Radicals. De Tocqueville, who became Foreign Minister in June 1849, wrote of his colleagues: "We wanted to call the Republic to life; the President wanted to bury it. We were his Ministers, but he wanted only accomplices." President Louis-Napoleon Bonaparte was working hard to make his office a permanency. Both he and the Assembly were due to retire in 1851. Failing to get the two-thirds majority necessary for the constitutional renewal of his term of office, Louis Bonaparte determined to outplay the demagogues at their own game. After touring the country in a series of wonderfully staged publicity campaigns, he prepared a *coup d'état* in Paris. On the night of 1 December 1851, his police arrested eighty Deputies in their beds and plastered the capital with proclamations announcing that there would be a new Constitution. No one need worry. There would be a free vote of the people to confirm or condemn the President's action—a plebiscite in which he would ask them whether or not they wanted him to continue as President for another ten years.

At first no one did worry. Then the few republicans who were still at large succeeded in arousing some sort of opposition. Barricades appeared in the streets again, once again to be swept away in the blood of working people, for Saint-Arnaud, whom Louis Napoleon (it is time to give him this name) had put at the head of the army, was popular with the troops. The masses were hardly stirred by the *coup*. Proudhon, taking a walk on his leave-day from prison, wrote of them: "When the pavements of the boulevards were still red with blood, I saw these good masses queueing for the theatres, content, joyful, quite without regret or remorse." The outside world was not interested. De Tocqueville, crying in the wilderness of the columns of the London *Times*, wrote on 11 December: "The liberty of the Press is destroyed, to an extent unheard of even in the time of the Empire. . . . As for the appeal to the people, to which Louis-Napoleon affects to submit his claims, never was a more odious mockery offered to a nation. . . . Force overcoming law, trampling on the liberty of the Press and of the person, deriding the popular will, in whose name the Government pretends to act —France torn from the alliance of free nations and yoked to the despotic monarchy of the continent— such is the result of the *coup d'état*. If the judgement of the people of England can approve this military saturnalia, I shall mourn for you and for myself and for the sacred cause of liberty throughout the world; for the public opinion of England is the grand jury of mankind in the cause of freedom, and if its verdict were to acquit the oppressor, the oppressed would have no other recourse but to God."

The plebiscite went, as plebiscites usually go, in favour of the man who organized it. On 20 December seven million Frenchmen confirmed Louis-Napoleon's tenure of office for a further ten years. The people of France had spoken. It remained for Proudhon to point the moral. "You still believe in the people," he wrote to Madier-Montjau in December 1852. "It is absolutely necessary that you should rid yourself of this false creed. We must serve liberty and morality for their own sakes . . . without despising the people, who are only savages and whom it is our duty to civilize, and without making them our sovereign. . . . How many times in these last five years have I caught the people in adultery, in indifference, in imperialist complicity, in ingratitude towards its teachers! Ah, the people have not deceived me; but cowardice, even when anticipated, is always hideous to see. I shall belabour the people, I warn you, until I have made the dogma of its alleged sovereignty fly into pieces. It is not enough that we should not see the incapable leaders of 1848 again; the thing is that we should not reconstruct their idol."

In Proudhon's view the political events of December 1851 were decisive: they put Louis-Napoleon firmly in the saddle for fifteen to twenty years. Granted that the tyrant was irremovable, what remained to be done? First, count your blessings: the idol of the political sovereignty of the masses had been proved to have feet of clay—that was one good thing. Second, attempt to turn the tyranny to good account. For a time Proudhon thought it not impossible that Louis-Napoleon could be converted to the ideas of economic self-government. Failing that, there might still be room under the tyranny to educate the masses, to teach them true doctrines, to bring out their inherent virtues. There was still work ahead for a man with a mission and a pen.

In the spring of 1852 the end of Proudhon's prison sentence was drawing near. "I shall be set free in thirty-eight days from now. I have so much on hand, am so comfortable at Ste. Pélagie for working, and know that being free will make so little change in my habits, that I look forward to the time with the most complete indifference." Other prisoners within sight of their release have often expressed the same sentiments: it is not prison life that is unendurable—man can adapt himself to anything—but the prospect of never getting out. Proudhon's release, whatever he may have said about it in anticipation, was to mark the chief turning-point of his life.

On 4 June Proudhon was set at liberty. He spent the whole long summer day walking with his wife and friends, like a good bourgeois, in the Bois de Meudon, with halts for two enormous meals. They planned to take a long holiday in the village of Burgille near Besançon; it would be a delight for them all and a necessity for the children, who had had a mild attack of smallpox. But first Proudhon had a job to finish : he had to get his latest book published. *La Révolution sociale demontrée par le Coup d'État du 2 decembre* was the last fruit of his prison period, ripened by the plebiscite. It was a call to Louis-Napoleon to fulfil the mission of France by basing his régime on mutual credit and on the reduction of interest rates, and a call to the lower middle classes—the natural champion of liberty, as opposed to the upper middle class of capitalists, the natural champions of authority—to fulfil their mission by leading the proletariat to emancipation. It was not a very revolutionary book, but no publisher dared touch it. Proudhon wrote to the Minister of the Interior for assurance against prosecution, but with no success. Then he wrote to Louis-Napoleon himself. "If there was one man with a head and a heart, just one, in the Government of 2 December, my work would go through. Must I go as far as you, Monsieur le Président, to find that man?" Flattered, Louis-Napoleon gave his permission. Garnier published the *Social Revolution* in July, and the Proudhon family went happily away for their holiday in the Franche Comté.

When they came back, at the end of October, they

moved into a flat in the Rue d'Enfer (later to be the Rue Denfert-Rochereau) at the end near the Conservatoire. It was a pleasant ground-floor apartment, facing south, with a big garden. Madame Proudhon adored it and developed a formidable house-pride, as well she might, having had no real home since her marriage. Proudhon settled down. He had never been a Bohemian and, although he could never be altogether a bourgeois, he was essentially a creature of order and routine and of fixed affections, and had a great need of a home and family life. For too long he had been a vagabond and a prisoner; henceforth he would live as the family man which he had always known himself to be.

The year 1852 also marked the turning-point in Proudhon's career as a writer. "From 1839 to 1852 I have had what might be called my *period of criticism*," he wrote. "Now I am preparing to begin a new period, which I will call, if you like, my *positive period*, a period of construction. It will last as long as the first, that is, thirteen to fourteen years." The forecast is remarkable, both for its accuracy and its inaccuracy. Proudhon was to die in 1865, but the fourteen years of constructive thinking and writing were not half enough for the work he had set himself.

So far he had published his criticism of property and of finance, of socialism and of capitalism, of democracy and of demagogy; they were negative except in so far as they contained sketches of a new economic basis laid in free credit, and of a new social basis founded on anarchy, and hints at an underlying philosophy of society. What was needed now was to work out in depth this underlying philosophy. Once this were done, it would remain only to apply the key-principle to each manifestation of social disease, from war and nationalism to libertinism and divorce. The series of books on applications would need vast research, but they would follow naturally from the fundamental work on principles. But where was this fundamental work to begin? The more he had read and studied economics and history, the more acutely he felt that there must be a key to the apparent contradiction, accidents and caprices of social phenomena. The key could not lie in the idea of an Absolute, of a Revelation—that was an error which had chronically blocked the search for truth. Truth could be discovered only through the conception of what Proudhon called—somewhat misleadingly—Progress. In a book written in prison but not published until 1853, and then in Brussels, Proudhon outlined this conception. "All ideas are false, that is to say, contradicting or irrational, if they are taken in an exclusive or absolute sense. All ideas are true, that is to say susceptible of being realized and useful, if they are taken in composition with others, or in evolution." Progress lies in progression, in the way in which new ideas extend the curve of knowledge, include the old truths in the sense of transcending their partial and transitory elements, and form an ever-widening circle of comprehension. The whirling sphere of Progress is held in its orbit by the pull of conflicting forces; their tension results in an equilibrium which has the balance of a dance. "There is nothing beyond or beneath this eternal dance. And the rhythm which controls it, the pure form of being, the supreme to which no particular manifestation of reality can ever approximate, is the highest conception which human reason can ever attain."

All this was too vague—a profession of faith, as

the author admitted, rather than a reasoned philosophy. Proudhon must now isolate the fundamental forces in each of the main fields of the science of society. "I have not ceased working on the nature of economics," he wrote to Bergmann in 1854, "that science which has not yet been defined . . . Side by side with economics, simultaneously and through it, I am studying history, and I have come to the conclusion that history, illuminated with a new understanding, will become in itself a new world to be explored." Proudhon projected a whole series of volumes on each subject, to be undertaken with the aid of collaborators. The work on history was to be called *Chronos* in echo of von Humbolt's *Cosmos*.

Neither the work on economics nor that on history appeared in the form that Proudhon first intended. For all his talk of science, he was inescapably a moralist, and inspiration deserted him as soon as he put off the prophet's mantle. The moral significance of social life was what really interested him. Slowly he came to see that two conflicting conceptions of human nature were at war for the domination or for the release—it comes to the same thing—of men's minds: the conception of justice, which Proudhon identified historically with the Revolution, and that of revelation, which he identified with the Church. The working out of this idea would be his *magnum opus*, his exposure of an underlying philosophy. For a long time he fumbled for a form, but by March 1855 he was writing in a letter : "I am engaged on a book, already well advanced, of 500 to 600 pages, which will squarely pose the whole question of religion. Because they won't want to print it in Paris—thanks to the influence of the clergy, which rules as well as reigns—I shall publish it in Belgium, taking care not to say anything that will shock our Government or even give any pretext for calling it an attack on religion. . . . Its title will be 'De la Morale dans le socialisme et dans l'Eglise, lettre à Monseigneur Césaire Mathieu, Cardinal Archevêque de Besançon.' . . . The real object will be to state with all force and thoroughness the *moral problem* of the Church and the Revolution, as Rousseau in 1760-2, replying to the Archbishop of Paris, Christophe de Beaumont, posed the question of revelation and miracles."

For the achievement of the great work which Proudhon had set himself on his release from prison, all that was needed was health and a little money. He was denied both. In the autumn of 1853, a few weeks after the birth of his third daughter, Stéphanie, the whole family were attacked by cholera. Marcelle died of it and the baby never wholly recovered from its after-effects; Stéphanie was delicate and ailing all through her childhood. Proudhon himself lost several precious months of work, and was left with a cerebral affection which attacked him intermittently for the rest of his days. Poverty as well as disease haunted the *ménage*. Only two of Proudhon's books—the *Confessions* and the *Révolution sociale*—had been a financial success; there was nothing to live on but advances from Garnier's, the Paris publishers. "Could you get me a place as a clerk at 4,000 francs a year?" Proudhon wrote in desperation to Charles Edmond in 1852. (In this year Karl Marx, in London, had to borrow two pounds to pay for his daughter's coffin, and pawned his overcoat to raise the price of paper on which to write a pamphlet). Even in despair Proudhon had no difficulty in refusing, with a modesty that is a model for all poor men who have ever been bribed with a fortune, a subvention of 20,000 francs offered through the patronage of Prince Jérôme Bonaparte. He preferred to earn his living by hack-work, and brought out a couple of books which he hoped would keep the wolf from the door—an anonymous Manual for Speculators on the Exchange, and a Project for Reform in the Administration of the Railways—but the wolf still gnawed. There were old debts to liquidate, a brother to be helped, a young family to be brought up in disease-ridden Paris. In 1855 Madame Proudhon went out to work at her old trade of lace-making in order to balance the family budget. In the following year, however, that source of income ended : Madame Proudhon was pregnant again and in May a fourth daughter, Charlotte, was born. The child died in December, of what was called "teething trouble." It is difficult to believe that the acute poverty of the household and the consequent overwork and anxiety of the mother were not partly responsible. That year Proudhon's capacity for work was reduced to half, according to his own estimate, by a return of the cerebral trouble which brought on acute headaches, fainting and a high fever. Illness is apt to bring panic to a man without employment, property or pension who has to live from month to month by selling the work of his brain. Friends would have helped him, but he always refused. He even insisted on paying for a present of Bordeaux wine, of which he might well have taken a little for his stomach's sake. The following year, 1857, brought neither better health nor more money. The headaches and fever persisted, and the whole of Proudhon's working hours went into unremunerative labour on his *magnum opus*.

It was finished at last. The great work was published in three weighty volumes on 22 April 1858, with the title significantly changed to *Justice in the Revolution and the Church: new principles of practical philosophy, addressed to Monsignor Césaire Mathieu, Cardinal Archbishop of Besançon (De la Justice dans la Révolution et dans l'Eglise: nouveaux principes de philosophie pratique, adressés, etc.).* Justice in the Revolution and the Church! Proudhon had found the guiding principle, the principle that held the human mind in its orbit.

Justice, which Proudhon had defined in his early essay on property as "recognition in others of a personality equal to one's own," is now given a fuller definition: "It is the respect for human dignity in whatever form or in whatever circumstances it may be compromised and at whatever risk one may expose oneself to by defending it." Rights consist in the faculty of securing this respect for others; duty consists in the obligation to recognize it oneself. The object of society is to achieve justice; the problem of society is to recognize rights and duties. Until the first French Revolution the problem was not within sight of solution; it was brought within sight by the concept of Equality, by which man took the achievement of justice into his own hands instead of relying on authority and revelation, ecclesiastical and monarchical. Political economy, which until then had been purely descriptive, now became for him a moral science.

The author went on to deduce from this principle of justice the application of morality to economics. Between employers and employees justice is to be established by recognizing that wages must be equivalent to the value produced by the worker; between borrowers and lenders by the institution of free credit. Economic rent is unjust : there is no justification for paying rent to the property-owner as such; it should be paid in part to the workers, in part to the community. The application of morality to politics rests on a similar system of equilibrium. Between the interests of the community and those of the individual, the balance is inevitably destroyed by centralized authority. Government upsets the economic balance, which can be achieved only by free federation of social groups—by Anarchism. The line of progress for the Revolution lies through the establishment of morality in economics and politics to the reform of individual morals. These two reforms are, of course, interconnected at every stage, but the point of application of individual morality is in the institution of marriage. Here Proudhon replies to a criticism of Herzen who had written : "Passion is intrinsically unjust; justice is remoter from the personal; it is impersonal—passion is only individual." Proudhon insisted that passion is reciprocal and that marriage is its social form : woman is the indispensable auxiliary of man in the service of justice, and the family is the transmitter both of individual and of social morality. "The organ of justice is the androgyne, or the conjugal couple," and when, through the couple, justice has been affirmed, sanctioned and guaranteed, the Revolution can be said to have been accomplished.

Justice, however, has a formidable enemy, and that enemy is the Church. . . . By proclaiming that all justice is in God, the Church made it transcendental and sanctioned a stultifying oppression of the individual. The Revolution made justice immanent, proclaiming that it is innate in man, progressing through society which man develops and perfects in the light of his sense of liberty. The Christian doctrines of the Fall, of Original Sin, of Authority and of Revelation are stultifying to conscience and therefore to justice. The Church is immoral in so much as it upholds an absolute ideal; any absolute, any mysticism, must be a negation of morality. Led astray by its mysticism, the Church tends to deny sexuality, to minimize woman and passion, and thus to destroy true marriage. The issue lies, therefore, between the principles of transcendance and immanence, between the Revolution and the Church. "Transcendentalism, in positing God, the supreme ideal, as the principle of practical reason, as the revealer and guarantor of justice, has ended by making the cult of this ideal into the destroyer of human dignity—by setting up Predestination and Grace in a negation of equality, by Providence in a fanaticism of *raison d'État*, by probabilism in the corruption of scholarship and the hypocrisy of science, by spiritualism in the enslavement of the workers, by the duplicity of conscience in moral doubt, by quietism in the inertia of the masses, given over like flocks to the consummation of their pastor; by hatred of Nature, fear of Hell and promise of Paradise to wretchedness in life and cowardice in face of death."

*Ecrasez l'infame!* Proudhon was writing in the true tradition of the precursors of the Revolution, and it is not surprising that in the Catholic Empire of Napoleon III and the Empress Eugénie the authorities should have found the book subversive. If they had considered it carefully (no easy task, for the book is a complex mixture of metaphysics and personal reminiscence) they would have found that this heir of Voltaire and Diderot was an upholder of traditional morality, at least as much opposed to the "progressives" as to the ecclesiasts, and that his anarchism was rooted in a social passion for order. "Morality [*la morale*]," they would have read, "is a revelation that society, the collectivity, makes the man, the individual. It is impossible to deduce morality either from hygiene or from economics or from metaphysics or from theology, as the materialists, the utilitarians, the dogmatic Christians, the Bossuets, etc., have successively tried to do. Morality comes from something different. This different thing, which some call conscience, some practical reason, etc., is as I see it, the *Social Essence*, the collective being which contains us and penetrates us, and which by its influence, its revelation, makes up the constitution of our soul." But all that was too difficult for police officials. Much easier to ban the book.

Proudhon's great work was seized by the police six days after its publication by Garnier's. The author was not dismayed. Writing to his Besançon friend Maurice a week or so later, he said: "The clamour of the clergy has got my book seized. . . . Of the 6,500 copies printed, only about 500 have been confiscated. . . . In short, the success of the book surpasses both our hopes and the expectation of the public. It puts me in an incomparable position and gives me a place far above any consequences that a trial may bring."

In this Proudhon was mistaken. The "public" had expected little from the book, for the simple reason that they had almost forgotten about him. The hero of 1848, who had played every revolutionary rôle— insurrectionist, journalist, Deputy of the Left, prisoner—had lost the ear of the public since the suppression of his last regular newspaper, *La Voix du Peuple*, in 1850. Herzen had written then: "The only man in France who still had something to say had no choice but to be silent." For six years he had been silent, except for a couple of pot-boilers and the little-read, Brussels-published *Philosophie du Progrès*. Meditating on the reasons for the neglect of Proudhon by his own people, the Russian Herzen put his finger on the weak spot of the French mind. "The French seek experimental solutions in him, and, finding no plans for the phalanstery nor for the Icarian community, shrug their shoulders and lay the book aside. . . . Proudhon is the first of a new set of French thinkers. His work marks a transition period, not only in the history of socialism, but also in the history of French logic. He has more strength and freedom in his argumentative tendency than the most talented of his fellow countrymen. Intelligent and single-minded men like Pierre Leroux and Considérant do not grasp either his point of departure or his method. They are accustomed to play with ideas as with marked cards, to walk in a certain attire along a beaten track to familiar spots. Proudhon often presses on without hesitating to crush anything in his way; without fearing to destroy or to go too far. He has none of that sensitiveness, that rhetorical revolutionary chastity, that takes the place of Protestant pieties in the French. . . . And that is why he remains a solitary figure among his own people, rather alarming than convincing them. . . . He did not use the grand phrases, he did not spare the Old Believers of the Revolution, and for that reason the French look on him as an egoist, as an individualist, almost as a renegade and a traitor. . . . The genius of Proudhon is really anti-pathetic to the rhetorical French, his language is offensive to them. The Revolution developed its own special puritanism, narrow and intolerant, its own obligatory jargon, and patriots resent anything not written in the official form, just as Russian judges do. . . . An original mind is hateful to them, they dislike original ideas as in the past."

When Proudhon went before the Court of the Police Correctionelle of the Department of the Seine and was condemned on 2 June 1858, and sentenced to a fine of 5,000 francs, and to three years' imprisonment, there was no body of public opinion in France to take up his cause. Condemned on five charges each more vague than the last—(i) Outrages against public and religious morality and attacks against the rights of the family; (ii) defending actions defined as crimes or offences by the penal law, (iii) attacks against the respect due to the law; (iv) exciting contempt or hatred between citizens; (v) publishing false news in bad faith—Proudhon lodged an appeal and fled to Brussels.

Not that he thought of his retreat to Belgium either as flight or exile. He insisted that he had gone to Brussels in order to publish there a *Mémoire* stating the grounds of his case to be presented before the Court of Appeal. Until that court should condemn him, there could be no question of exile. His intention was to establish the right to a written defence; as soon as it was established, he would return. But of course the *Mémoire* was prohibited, and Proudhon, who had taken temporary lodgings at 22 Rue du Chemin-de-fer under the name of "M. Durfort, Professeur de Mathématiques," stayed on in Belgium.

So the post-prison period of Proudhon's life culminated in separation from his country, his public and his friends. After six years of freedom, years passed in poverty and felicity, in physical sickness and intellectual health, he found himself in an isolation more severe than any that he had known in prison. Those six years had sufficed for the gestation and production of his *magnum opus*; exile must suffice for the rest of the task that he had set himself in 1852.

## Chapter Seven

# The Fifties

FOR Marx the decade between 1849 and 1859 was to be the most wretched and unproductive in his life. When he came to London at the age of thirty-one, he had no friends, no money and no prospects. He found lodgings for his family in a German hotel in Leicester Square, but soon they had to move out because of the expense. The only home he could afford was a two-room flat in Dean Street. In those two rooms the family had to live for six years —Marx, Jenny, their servant Lenchen Delmuth and the children. At first there were three children— Jenny, Laura and Edgar; then, a month after their arrival in London, a fourth child, Guido, was born; a year later came a fifth, Franziska; four years later a sixth, Eleanor; and Jenny was to be pregnant a seventh time, but the child was stillborn. Only three of the six children survived those years in Soho. Guido and Francesca died in infancy, and Edgar, the only surviving son and Marx's particular darling, died at the age of nine, in 1855.

We know only too well what those Dean Street rooms looked like. A Prussian spy gave his Government a description of them : "There is not one clean or decent piece of furniture in either room, everything is broken, tattered and torn, with thick dirt over everything. . . . Manuscripts, books and newspapers lie beside the children's toys, bits and pieces from the wife's sewing-basket, cups with broken rims, dirty spoons, knives and forks, lamps, an inkpot, tumblers, pipes, tobacco-ash—all piled up on the same table. On entering the room, smoke and tobacco fumes make your eyes water to such an extent that you seem to be groping about in a cavern—until you get used to it and manage to make out certain objects in the haze. Sitting down is a dangerous business. Here is a chair with only three legs, there another which happens to be whole, on which the children are playing at cooking. That is the one that is offered to the visitor, but the children's cooking is not removed, and if you sit down on it you risk a pair of trousers."

Marx and his wife were not Bohemians; they were respectable, socially conventional bourgeois who had been brought up in a degree of comfort amounting to luxury. They felt their poverty to be degrading and disgusting, but they did not allow it to sour their family life. The spy goes on to say: "But all these things do not in the least embarrass Marx or his wife. You are received in the most friendly way and are cordially offered pipes, tobacco and whatever else there may happen to be. Presently a clever and interesting conversation arises which makes up for all the domestic deficiencies and makes the discomfort bearable."

Life in Soho might have been a great deal more easily bearable if Marx could have brought himself to mix with the other revolutionary exiles who were in London at that time. Mazzini was there and Kossuth the Hungarian, and Herzen and a circle of Russians, and Louis Blanc and the Pole Worcell. Marx shut himself off from them all. The only company he could easily stand was that of Germans, and with them he spent most of his time quarrelling. Only Engels remained his friend, and Engels was in Manchester working the Lancashire branch of his father's business, and held by that gentleman on such tight purse-strings that there was little he could save to send to Marx in the way of money. Engels gave Marx everything else—friendship, confidence, respect, collaboration—and it was on Engels that Marx depended, in a sense deeper than the financial, during those sad Soho years.

For a living Marx had to find odd jobs of hack journalism. His first real chance in the journalistic field did not come till 1851, when Charles A. Dana asked him to send a couple of articles a week to the *New York Tribune*, offering five dollars for every article that was printed. This was a great opportunity. The *New York Tribune*, founded by Horace Greely, had become the organ of the Fourierists after the breakdown of the Brook Farm Community. Dana was a Fourierist and had been a member of the community. The paper was influential and successful; it had a circulation bigger than any other in the world. The only trouble about the assignment from Marx's point of view was that articles must be in English, and Marx's command of that language was not yet sufficient to allow him to write in it. Luckily there was Engels : for the first year and frequently after that Marx's articles were written by Engels, either from Marx's notes or entirely out of his own head. The series went on for ten years and Dana raised no trouble about the articles submitted, though it was rarely that he printed more than one a week and sometimes a whole month passed without the appearance of a single article signed by Marx. There were some magnificent articles among them, particularly

those by Engels on military matters, and those by
Marx on English domestic politics and English rule
in Ireland and India.

But the best of Marx's journalistic writings of this
period were on France. They were published in two
volumes entitled respectively *The Civil War in
France* and *The 18th Brumaire of Louis Bonaparte*.
They were brilliant, excitingly-written essays in
which Marx used his economic interpretation of history as a fine cutting-tool for the delineation of an
event in current history. He was particularly pleased
with *The 18th Brumaire*, which he thought much
superior to Proudhon's work on the same subject:
"Proudhon's *Coup d'État* attempts to show the coup
as the result of a train of previous historical development, but in his hands the historical construction of
the coup develops into an historical apologia for its
hero. In my treatment of the subject, however, I
show how the class struggle in France created conditions and circumstances which made it possible for a
mediocre and grotesque individual to play the part
of a hero."

If the pamphlets on French politics were among
the best of Marx's journalistic writing, those on
Russia were among the worst. As a Jew, a German
and a champion of the working-class, he had always
been a Russophobe, and in the pieces later published
under the titles of *Palmerston, What Has He Done?*
and *The Secret Diplomacy of the Eighteenth Century*, the hatred of Russia amounted to a mania. In
this he found an ally and a patron in a crazy Scots-
man, David Urquhart, who strangely enough was
the only colleague except Engels with whom he never
quarrelled. Among English revolutionaries he had
two colleagues at this time, survivors of the left-wing

of the Chartist Movement. With one of these, Harvey, a seaman's son who had been on the staff of the *Northern Star* and who started a paper of his own, the *Red Republican*, in which he published a translation of the *Communist Manifesto*, Marx soon parted company; but with the other, Ernest Jones, a German-educated eccentric, he got on rather better until it became clear that Jones would not accept Marx's dictatorship on every point of policy.

Of all this journalistic writing nothing except the articles in the *New York Tribune* brought in any money, and nothing, except perhaps *The 18th Brumaire*, gave him much satisfaction. He was supposed to be writing a serious work on political economy, a work which he had had in mind ever since the Brussels days, and of which some beginnings had appeared in the polemic against Proudhon, the *Misère de la Philosophie*. But always something got in the way. Partly it was Marx's own temperament. As Engels told him in 1851 : "So long as there is a book in front of you which you consider important and which you haven't read, you don't put pen to paper." Marx seemed incurably inhibited when it came to writing, and his long vigils in the British Museum Library produced tomes of notes and extracts but never a page of his own book. It was always easier to throw off a newspaper article or to plunge into a polemic. Partly, too, his failure to get on with his book was due to illness and family trouble. He suffered abominably from hæmorrhoids and from an obscure disease of the liver. The death of his son Edgar in the spring of 1855 was the worst blow of his life. "It is impossible to describe how much we miss him all the time," he wrote to Engels. "I have suffered all sorts of misfortune, but now I know what real suffering is. . . . In all the terrible anxiety and suffering I have gone through I have been sustained by the thought of you and your friendship, and by the hope that we still have something worth-while to do together in the world."

The summer of 1855 brought an improvement in the family's material condition. Jenny's mother died, and her estate, together with a legacy from Jenny's Scottish relatives, made it possible to leave the Soho rooms and to move into a house on Haverstock Hill (9 Grafton Terrace). "Compared with the holes we have previously had to live in," wrote Jenny Marx, "this is a really princely house, and though everything we possess cost little more than £40—much of it second-hand rubbish—I felt myself grand in our new parlour at first. All the linen and the other reminders of our former glory were recovered from the hands of Uncle, and once again I was able to count over my old damask napkins with delight. However, the idyll did not last for very long, for soon one piece after the other found its way back to the 'pop-shop' (as the children will call the house at the sign of the mysterious three brass balls). Still, we were very happy in our agreeable bourgeois cosiness."

Whether it was the bourgeois cosiness which made Marx able to settle down to serious writing we do not know, but in 1856 he was at work on a book and in 1859 it was published. This was not the *magnum opus* that he had intended; the *Critique of Political Economy* was a fragment containing a mere couple of chapters dealing largely with the labour theory of value. The *Critique* attracted no attention, and soon Marx was off in the more congenial direction of polemics. A Swiss Radical, Karl Vogt, had suggested that Marx had left his colleagues of the Communist

League in the lurch in Cologne; Marx set about wiping the floor with Vogt, whom he accused of being in the pay of the French Emperor, in a book written in 1860 under the telling title of *Herr Vogt*.

It was a poor end to a poor decade in Marx's life and in the life of the working-class movement. While *Herr Vogt* was being published Jenny was laid up with small-pox, and her doctor was telling Marx that the illness would probably save her from a mental breakdown. The book itself did not save the family from a financial breakdown. It sold eight copies in England, and the publisher failed to distribute it in Germany; Marx was left to defray the total cost of printing.

Meanwhile Proudhon was in exile in Belgium. In December 1858, having borrowed money for their fare, he was joined by his wife and two daughters in Brussels, where he had found a flat in the Ixelles suburb. It was small and dark, and there was no garden. There was not even a study for the philosopher, who had to work amid the food and linen in a tiny store-room. Madame Proudhon was in despair : there was so much to do, so much dirt and everything was strange. A Parisian who had never been out of Paris except for a rare holiday, she could not reconcile herself to foreign parts and ways. Above all, she missed her furniture, especially the bed, which had been left behind in the Rue d'Enfer because removal would have been expensive. Proudhon, however, was full of hope. Near his fiftieth birthday—on 11 January 1859—we find him writing a letter buoyant with plans for the future : "After nearly twenty years of criticism and logic, I have published a work, *La Justice,* which contains for

the first time the whole of my affirmations. . . . Now
is the time to *popularise* all that—in other words, to
pay it out in small change . . . I am starting, under
the provisional title of *Popular Philosophy*, an in-
definite series of publications on all sorts of subjects
—history, literature, political economy, ethics, biography, etc."

He was thinking of beginning with a work of
literary criticism which would be an attack on
Michelet's recently published *l'Amour*, and on the
contemporary novels which Proudhon called the
"literature of fornication." Writing in March to
Chaudey, the counsel who was in charge of his case,
he said : "This school of descriptive, emphatic, de-
clamatory, sensibility-mongering writers, culminat-
ing in the *Mystères de Paris*, in the novels of George
Sand, in frothy journalism, etc., this now decimated
school ought to give place to another which will
better represent the French genius—grave, sober,
rising above love, idealism and enthusiasm, and refusing to admit poetry and eloquence unless they are
stiffened by a strong dose of common sense, malice,
sang-froid and wit. . . . That, under the names of
Voltaire and Diderot, will be the subject of my
book."

He was also contemplating a book on foreign politics, which, as he said, would be a "highly unexpected
development of the fundamental principles of *La
Justice*." He had never before given much attention
to foreign affairs, but now sojourn in a foreign land,
combined with the prospect of a French war of intervention in Italy, forced him to examine them. As
usual, he started with first principles, asking himself
where the basis of the rights of nations lay and what
constituted the moral justification of war. "Current

events having called my attention to international politics," he wrote to Chaudey in June, "I asked myself what this policy is, what principle it is based on, what philosophy lies behind it, and I have found that it has no principle—either in France or anywhere else. I have consulted the authorities—Grotius, for instance: they show a great deal of erudition, a sense of tradition and custom, but as for principles—nothing. Grotius shook the branch of knowledge (in *De Jure belli ac pacis*), but he could not make any fruit fall."

Proudhon's mind was working hard, but his body refused collaboration. Throughout 1859 he enjoyed hardly a single month of uninterrupted good health. A bad attack of influenza incapacitated him in the spring, and summer brought, not the improvement he expected, but a relapse. This time, the whole family caught the disease, and there was no one but the father to do the housework and the nursing while the little girls and the mother were in bed. In the autumn Stéphanie had a bad attack of scarlatina which turned to hydropsy and nearly cost her her life. It was an appalling year. Proudhon could do no work at all for six months and not a sou was coming in. Worse than that, he was getting into debt. A book written for a Belgian publisher proved unsatisfactory when he saw it in proof and he withdrew it, compensating the publishers with 1,000 francs out of his own pocket. His brother Charles in the Franche Comté was in deep water, and Proudhon saved him from his creditors by an allowance, scraped together goodness knows how. He begged an advance in royalties from Garnier. He borrowed from Beslay. It all worried him a great deal: "I am in debt," he complained again and again in letters.

One wonders why Proudhon did not go to England. London was proverbially kind to political refugees. Louis Blanc, Ledru-Rollin and other 1848 leaders were there; Herzen's house in Hampstead was a home for dozens of eminent exiles of all nationalities, and Herzen's purse, open to so many, could never have been closed to Proudhon, whom he admired more than anybody. And Proudhon had some appreciation of England : "It has for centuries been the way of that country that everything works together for good because it is free and because, as soon as the well-being of the nation is threatened, the whole people becomes unanimous," he had written in January 1859. Yet perhaps the reasons why he did not think of going to London are not far to seek. Not only was it too distant and expensive; it was also too foreign. Though he had been to Belgium and to Switzerland before, Proudhon had never been out of a French-speaking country. The French way of life was as necessary to him as air—one almost said as wine, of which he drank little, from principle and from necessity, but which he needed to taste daily. Also he sensed that there would be something peculiarly foreign to him in England, "where no one reads me."

In 1860 the clouds began to lift a little. Proudhon was in better health and was writing at the top of his bent. The book on literature began to come into focus. He saw now that it would have to be two books —neither of them on literature indeed, because belles-lettres bored him profoundly. There would have to be one on Woman and one on the tradition of Voltaire and the Encyclopédistes. The book on international affairs would also have to be two : one treating on the theme of War and another on the nature of Nationalism. All these would be applications of the general principles enunciated in *La Justice*. That book was the key to them all. Not satisfied with the original edition, Proudhon set about re-writing it for a second, enlarged edition which a Belgian publisher had agreed to bring out in twelve instalments.

All these were long-term projects. They would not bring in a sou for the current year. But the Swiss Canton of Vaud, neighbouring the Franche-Comté, was offering a prize of 1,550 francs for an essay on Taxation, and Proudhon was sure that he could win it. He had a lot to say about fiscal principles, and he dashed off a book. Altogether he wrote the equivalent of fifteen hundred printed pages in that year, counting the additions to *La Justice*. Yet nothing was published; there was no revenue. Proudhon had borrowed 1,000 francs from Garnier in December 1859; a year later his debts to Charles Beslay reached a similar sum. "I have told you that these last years, 1858, 1859, 1860, have been disastrous for me," he wrote to Beslay, "the first because of the condemnation of my book which forced me into exile and an expensive removal; the second through illnesses and the sheer loss of a thousand francs over an attempted publication which I was obliged to suppress; the third through the re-printing of my book—a new edition which, for the present at least, will bring me in very little." But there was no real need to worry: Garnier and Beslay were rich men and could wait for their money in their belief in Proudhon; and indeed every franc would be repaid. The news of his amnesty, which was announced on 12 December, was an anti-climax. It made no difference whatever to Proudhon's preoccupations. He could go back to

France when he would. He would go back when he was not so poor, when he was not so busy, when . . . but, really, how could he think of that now with so much on his hands?

The year 1861 brought some recognition. The Canton de Vaud awarded its prize to Proudhon, and the essay was published in September under the title of *La Théorie de l'Impôt* (*The Theory of Taxation*). Meanwhile he had at last found a publisher for the book on war. (Dentu brought it out after Hetzel and Garnier had refused. Proudhon could not understand Garnier's refusal, although the wretched man had been fined a thousand francs and sent to prison for publishing *La Justice*.) *La Guerre et la Paix* brought Proudhon recognition of a type which he had not expected. He was hailed as a reactionary, a renegade, a war-monger, and not, it must be admitted, without some superficial justification, for the pages were full of Proudhonian paradox, and contained sentences which, isolated from their context, would be enough to ruin any humanitarian writer.

It is easy to be a pacifist on paper, easy to write variations on the theme that war is evil. But war is, and always has been, a social fact; and as such it demands explanation as well as denunciation. True to his nature, Proudhon went to the roots of war, and found it to be a manifestation of the right of force which is the historical foundation of all society, all legislation, the foundation of all social rights, as well as of slavery, serfdom and property. With the coming of democracy the right of force was transformed into the right of numbers, the right of the majority. And at the same time other rights were being established—the right to work and to its produce, the right to opinions and knowledge and to their expression.

War was no longer a means of achieving social ends; it had become, like the Church, an anachronism. It would be a long time before mankind would realize this, and in the meanwhile a system of guarantees, internationally agreed, would be needed to regulate war and to promote peace.

The first part of *La Guerre et la Paix* contains the most striking philosophical vindication of war that has ever been written. Many were the readers who never got beyond this first part, and were shocked beyond measure at Proudhon's apparent change of front. In fact, he had not deviated an inch from his course. He expected his readers to understand this. In October 1861, he wrote to an anonymous correspondent: "I can see now that people are telling you, and you are beginning to believe, that I am taking a step backwards. You must let them say what they like and try to understand me, instead of getting alarmed. I am the only writer who, since the *coup d'état*, has made any progress in the direction of the Social Republic, which I am striving to endow with an *economic science* and with a *general philosophy*. And now, because for the last ten years I have taken a new line, because I have left polemics aside in order to plunge into general ideas, you tell me, echoing the calumniators and their gang, that I am turning into a *moderate*, a *conservative*!" Proudhon had, in fact, never been anything else. He had always attacked the self-styled revolutionaries, and now that Bakunin, Mazzini and the rest were preaching war for all they were worth, it was time to attack them more roundly than ever—to attack with a broad philosophical sweep which would show them that the justification of war was not confined to the red shirt of the warrior. He knew that it was necessary to the progress of what he understood as the Revolution to be a conservative, but in his own peculiar interpretation of that word, which no one who did not thoroughly understand his thought must ever make use of. "My ambition is, after having been the most revolutionary thinker of my time, to become, without changing my opinions one iota, the *most conservative*," he wrote to Beslay. Who would understand this? Behind his immoderate language, he had always been a hater of violence; behind his insistence on Revolution, always a conserver of what he conceived to be the basic institutions of mankind.

Marriage and the family he had always held to be the most fundamental of all. He had written books, still unpublished, on the subject. More exceptionally, he practised, in the poky Brussels flat, what he preached. His wife—become a demon, as he admitted, through overwork, illness and penury—was the only woman in his life. His daughters were his abiding delight, and he was avid as a peasant for their settlement in marriage. When a M. Neveu proposed an eventual match between his son and Proudhon's elder daughter, Proudhon replied in all seriousness: "It is not for me, the father of two daughters, to run after husbands. Let me add that we are still far from the event. Catherine is a good girl, quiet, affectionate, cheerful, but not precocious in any way. She has the nature of children of her age (she is ten today), but a good deal less than their mischievousness. On the whole, I don't look for the fashionable talents in her, so much as for good domestic work and decent feeling. She is beginning to be a real help to her mother, who has no servant and works like a galley-slave. A lady of our acquaintance gives a piano lesson to the two little girls every week; I permit it, not through any desire to see them become musicians, but so that they may learn to love music. That, my dear friend, is the position of your future daughter-in-law. Don't expect anything brilliant of her; count merely on a straightforward character, not without its little wilfulnesses. As for Stéphanie, the younger of my daughters, with a quite different disposition, a more attractive appearance and much more originality, she is not likely, I think, to surpass the elder; she has the same pitch, the same gamut, but a more difficult humour and perhaps less robust health." (One cannot help wondering which was the father's favourite. "Catherine," he wrote later to Neveu, "is lacking in vital energy but not in health. Stéphanie is a lion.")

Proudhon had settled down in Brussels as he had settled in prison and in the Rue d'Enfer. A year had passed since his amnesty had been granted, but he still made no move towards France. His future, he liked to think, was assured. In a letter to Maurice he wrote : "I think I can count now on a faithful public in Belgium, in Switzerland, in Germany, in Russia and everywhere abroad, except in England where no one reads me. In France, although my popularity is waning among the social democrats, the learned public receive me better than formerly; altogether I reckon I can rely on an average of 3,000 buyers. Such is my situation. With that I think I can not only live and bring up my daughters, but pay all my debts." Yet a doubt crept in, and later in the same letter he was writing : "It is only a question of working and producing. For that health and energy are needed, and there, I must confess, I begin to falter. Do you know how old I am ? Fifty-three on 15 January 1862. It's no longer a joke. I must make the best of what is left—ten years of good work, God willing, and after that I think I shall be able to take a rest."

But when would he return to France? In letter after letter he made excuses for postponing it; he had formed his habits; his children were in the middle of their school year; his wife was ill; he could not afford the removal and the journey. None of these was a true reason. The truth was that he could not apply his mind to leaving Brussels because he had a book on hand—and a very good book, *Majorats littéraires*, or *Writers' Copyright*, in which he was making a résumé of all his writings on Property, restating the famous antithesis between "Property is theft" and "Property is liberty," and showing the synthesis of the contradiction. And there was another reason, a hint at which creeps out in a letter written to Gouvernet at the end of 1861. "If it was a case of anyone other than I, the critics would go a bit deeper; they would speak with decency, they would examine motives; at the very least, they would enter into discussion. But I am still regarded as an eccentric writer, importunate, unaccommodating, unpleasant. I get kicks and pin-pricks; the women join in and there it goes. The Jacobin Democrats are angry with me; the Orleanists can't stand me; the Legitimists use me as a stick to beat their rivals with; the Bonapartists are content to keep silent. Sometimes a lost soul among the journalists launches an attack on me, but there is no echo. More than ever I ask myself if I am still of this world at all, whether I count or whether I ought to regard myself as a soul in torment who comes back to scare the living and those who refuse to pray for it. My success with the booksellers is enough for the support of my family and for my pride as an author; but I should like to have some influence on the march of events, and it is from that sphere that I feel myself excluded." Proudhon wanted to be welcome; he wanted to be useful. It was a forgivable ambition in a man of fifty-three who had all his life been a voice crying in the wilderness.

*Chapter Eight*

# The Awakening

WITH the 1860s came a political stirring which was to lift socialism out of the doldrums in which it had been becalmed since the 1848 revolutions. Europe now was in a careless rapture over nationalism. Everyone professing or calling himself a socialist or a liberal was in ecstasies over the Italian and Polish nationalist movements. Governments as far from the left as those of Napoleon III in France and of Palmerston in Britain were champions of national unity. In Italy French troops had helped Cavour to drive the Austrians out of Lombardy in 1859; enlightened public opinion everywhere had welcomed the nationalist revolution in the central Italian duchies in 1860; Garibaldi's conquest of Sicily and Naples and Cavour's penetration of the eastern Papal States united the workers of the world in praise. The hero of the working-classes everywhere was Garibaldi. As for Poland, the cause of her national unity and her liberation from Russia had become the symbol of liberty in general, so much so that the Poles were preparing a rising in the confident expectation of foreign intervention on their behalf. The only people who opposed the nationalist movement were the Romanovs, the Hapsburgs, the Bourbons and their minions—and Proudhon.

Socialists have never to this day made up their

minds about nationalism. The rank and file are still apt to get no further than thinking it a Good Thing because it frees people from foreign oppressors, and at the same time a Bad Thing because national states divide the workers from their foreign brothers and put the national bourgeoisie in power. The confusion dates from the early 1850s and from the lead given to socialist thought then by Marx and Proudhon.

Proudhon had always opposed nationalist movements for the same reason as he had opposed socialist movements : because they led to centralization and thence to the smothering of liberty and justice. More socialist than the socialists, he was also more nationalist than the nationalists. "I bow down to the spirit of nationalism as I do to that of the family : it is precisely for that reason that I protest against large political unities, which seem to be nothing but the confiscation of nationalities." United Italy would mean a corrupt, bureaucratic Italy. United Poland would mean a corrupt, imperialistic Poland. Back in 1857, he had written in *La Justice* : "The people like playing with big pieces: centralization, the indivisible Republic, the unitary Empire. For the same reason they like Communism. French unity, Italian unity, German unity, Scandinavian unity, unity everywhere—that's what goes down with the people and better still with the Government. Switzerland, a confederation of twenty-two little states, all sovereign, just does not exist for them." Now in newspaper articles and letters he was trying to make the masses see the error of their views before it was too late— before the Poles should have risen in hopeless revolt and been suppressed, before the Italians should have bound themselves to the bureaucracy of Cavour.

Proudhon was abundantly right, as the future

would show : right in detail, as when he pointed out that Napoleon III would never really allow Italian unity; right in general, as when he forecast the nature of the eventual Polish Republic and of the Italian Kingdom; right even in his paradoxes, as when he wrote : "The nations least fitted to be united are those which resemble each other most." But he was wrong in thinking that anyone could be persuaded by his arguments in 1862.

In September the storm burst upon Proudhon's head. A casual remark in a newspaper article was taken out of its context to imply that he was in favour of the annexation of Belgium to France. One evening —it was 11 September—a crowd gathered outside his house in the Rue du Conseil, waving flags and shouting up at Proudhon's windows "Long live Belgium ! Down with the Annexationists !" The police who dispersed the demonstrators advised Proudhon to make himself scarce for a few days. He slipped away to Spa, but next evening there was a second, uglier demonstration. This time the police had to close the Rue du Conseil, and the Belgian Government placarded the district with official warnings against disturbances. Proudhon returned from Spa on the 15th, made hasty arrangements for the security of his family, and two days later took the train for Paris, where he must find, furnish and equip a new home.

Thus virtual exile ended in virtual expulsion. After over four years, years which had seen the deterioration of his health and the development of his thought, years more barren of success and more fertile in work than any period of his life, the philosopher returned to Paris to escape the fury of a Brussels mob.

Proudhon was too busy to be bitter, too ill to be angry. He spent some time house-hunting in Paris, then went back to Brussels to pack up his manuscripts and household goods and to see to the removal of his family, and incidentally to face the music caused by the publication of a pamphlet on *La Fédération et l'Unité en Italie*. At last, on 28 October, they were all installed in the new flat, No. 10, Grande Rue, Passy, amid their smashed crates of furniture and broken crockery, the mother worn out, the children sick and the father exhausted but triumphant. They had a roof over their heads, a home. They were back, all together, in Paris. Proudhon's chronic catarrh had turned to asthma, but the crises of asthma do not last for ever and nobody had been known to die in one. There was no money, of course, and plenty of debts in Paris, but at least he owed nobody in Brussels anything—no, that was not quite true : "We find that we owe to the successor of Nadoun, the photographer in the Montague-de-la-Cour," he wrote hastily to the wealthy Delhasse, "the sum of one franc, which my wife did not have the time to take to him as she had meant to do. It is the only debt that we have left outstanding in Brussels. Would you be so kind, dear friend, as to pay this franc and to debit me with it till the next occasion ?"

Now for work. Proudhon knew that the fecundating part of his life's work was already done. He had conceived all his cardinal ideas; all that remained was to bring them to birth in literary form. The baggage that he brought back from Brussels contained the manuscript of no fewer than sixteen books, more or less complete, in notes, outlines or near-final draft. All that they needed was writing. He would begin with his work on Nationalism, partly because it was

the newest of his ideas as well as the most topical,
partly because it offered the best opportunity for a
summary of his thinking life. "Like you," he had
written to his oldest friend, Bergmann, in May 1862,
"while following the direction of my studies in obedi-
ence to my first impulsions and, it must be added, in
throwing myself at times into the controversies of the
day, I have a longing to sum myself up, to say in a
few pages, with clarity and simplicity, what I want,
what I believe, and what I am!"

After these months of "sweating blood and water
to give birth to a beastly brochure," Proudhon produced *Du Principe Fédératif*. It was an admirable
little book, the shortest of Proudhon's major works
and one of the best written. Although the latter half,
in which he plays ninepins with his critics, dates as
badly as a book by Marx, the first part stands not
only as the clearest summary of Proudhon's political
thought but also as the best exposition of the federal
principle that has ever been written.

The nationalist awakening of the early 1860s
never excited Marx to anything like the degree to
which it excited Proudhon. The forces of history in
Marx's view were making for ever larger political
units. If nationalist movements aimed at the setting
up of small states, they were an absurdity. If, as in
Germany, they meant the coalescence of small states
into a larger unit, they might with moderation be
welcomed. The only thing that really mattered was
the cause of the workers of the world : if a nationalist movement could be used tactfully to further that
cause, then the socialists should use it; if not, they
should despise nationalism and all its works.

It was a simple enough doctrine, and it is a pity
that Marx and Engels never worked it out in read-

able form. Their views on the subject are to be found in letters from which it is not altogether fair to quote, for there they gave rein to their German prejudices which they would surely have curbed in print. Marx, for instance, concurred when Engels wrote to him: "The more I reflect upon history, the more clearly I see that the Poles are completely finished as a nation, and that they can only be useful as a means to an end up to the time when Russia herself is drawn into the agrarian revolution. From that moment Poland will no longer have any *raison d'être* whatever. The Poles have never done anything in history but commit courageous, quarrelsome stupidities. It would be impossible to cite a single occasion when Poland, even as against Russia, has successfully represented progress or done anything whatever of historical significance." Marx's letters were even more outspoken. When the Franco-Prussian War started in 1870, he wrote to Engels: "The French need a thrashing. If the Prussians win, then the centralization of the *State power* will help the centralization of the German working-class. German preponderance, moreover, will shift the centre of gravity of the working-class movement of Western Europe from France to Germany"—and he added that that would mean "the preponderance of our theory over those of Proudhon, etc."

Proudhon's theories were nowhere laid down more clearly than in his *Du Principe Fédératif*. "Politics," he wrote, "rest fundamentally on two contrary principles—Authority and Liberty." The mistake has been to think of them as exclusive; in reality they are interdependent. "Take away one of the two, and the other has no meaning. Authority without liberty to discuss, resist or submit is an empty word. Liberty without an authority as a counter-weight is an empty word." Both must be recognized, and the only way of reconciling them is through a contract of federation. In becoming a citizen "it is necessary that each individual entering the association of the State (i) has as much to receive from the State as he sacrifices to it; (ii) retains the whole of his liberty, his sovereignty and his initiative except that part which relates to the special object for which the contract is made and for which he is asking the guarantee of the State." (Between this form of social contract and that of Rousseau he adds, in parenthesis, there is all the difference between reality and hypothesis.) Such a contract can only be made in a small community; Proudhon agrees with Aristotle that only small states can be free states. Subsequent development must be by federation between states. The Swiss Confederation has shown the way in its constitution of 1848. Each member-state retains sovereignty except over such functions as it has freely and specifically assigned to the Confederate Government. Only thus can Authority and Liberty be reconciled in a nation. Only thus can annexationism and aggressionism be ruled out between nations, for the Federated State is organized essentially for defence rather than for attack.

But political federation demands economic federation. "If the federal régime merely serves to protect capitalist and mercantile anarchy; if the production and distribution of wealth is left to chance; if, by the effect of this false anarchy, society finds itself divided into two classes, one of the landowners, capitalists and entrepreneurs, the other of salaried or wage-earning proletarians, one of the rich, the other of the poor—the political edifice will always be unstable."

What is needed is for the corporations to federate. "All industries are related. Seen separately, they are but dismemberments of each other. One cannot survive the ruin of another. Let them federate, then— not to absorb each other, not to merge, but to guarantee mutually the conditions of prosperity which apply to all of them and of which no one can claim the monopoly."

The sub-title of the book was *The Necessity of Reconstructing the Party of the Revolution*. Proudhon made out an overwhelming case against the central, unifying tradition started by the Jacobins, and carried on by republicans and social democrats of all countries and decades down to the contemporary Jules Favre, Mazzini and Garibaldi—the tradition which had made the party of the Revolution the abettor of Napoleons small and large, and of dynasties as various as the Orleanists, the Hohenzollerns and the House of Savoy. He urged that the party of the Revolution must be reconstructed as the party of decentralization, of Federation. "The cause of the proletariat and that of European equilibrium are one and the same; each protests with an equal energy against unity and in favour of the federal system."

The book was indeed Proudhon's last word on economic and social principles. He summarized them and threw out his final challenge in a single sentence. "All my economic ideas, elaborated during twenty-five years, can be summed up in these three words : Agricultural Industrial Federation; all my political ideas are reducible to a similar formula : Political Federation or Decentralization; and since I am not making my ideas into an instrument of party politics or a means of personal advancement, all my hopes of the present and the future are expressed in this third term, corollary to the two others : Progressive Federation. I defy anyone to make a profession of faith that is at the same time clearer, farther reaching and of greater moderation; I would even go further and defy any friend of liberty and right to refute that profession."

It was in "the centralization of the German working-class" that Marx was interested above all else in the early 1860s. A socialist movement had been revived in Germany by Friedrich Lassalle, and everything seemed to depend on the form and direction which Marx could give it. Lassalle was an old admirer of Marx : he had headed the subscription list for money to bring Marx from Paris to London in 1849 and had arranged for the publication of his books in Germany, and had given other proofs of his devotion by the attention and respect with which he listened to Marx's advice. But the personal characters and relations of the two men would make collaboration impossible, and that impossibility was to have grievous effects on the German working-class movement.

Lassalle was a Jew from Breslau, seven years younger than Marx, handsome, flamboyant and talented to the verge of genius. He once told Marx that he had been a revolutionary since 1843—which must have annoyed the older man, whose conversion had come very much later. Lassalle first came into the public eye by taking up the cause of a German princess who was trying to divorce her husband, the Count von Hatzfeldt. For eight years he fought for the cause of Sophie von Hatzfeldt, until he had won her her divorce and a very favourable financial settlement. Then he turned his energies to the cause of the German workers. They had been deprived of political representation since the failure of the 1848 revolution. Instead of universal suffrage there was now a system of votes according to income, which practically excluded the workers. Lassalle led the campaign for universal suffrage, and led it in a way that had never been attempted before. His method was to tour the country making speeches to audiences of factory workers. In Berlin he put before the factory audiences what he called a "Workers' Programme." He wanted Marx's advice on this, and he wanted Marx's collaboration in the founding of a new daily paper.

With this in view he succeeded in getting Marx to visit him in Berlin in 1861. It was a painful time for Marx, who was feasted on venison and provided with a box next to the royal box at the ballet. Lassalle's hope had been to get the authorities to give Marx permission to live in Germany; but this they would not do. Marx returned to London, where Lassalle visited him in the following year.

Lassalle's visit to London was more disastrous than Marx's visit to Berlin. Jenny wanted to entertain him as befitted a man of his lavish way of life, but the landlord was threatening to send the bailiffs into Grafton Terrace, and there was hardly money for food, let alone for wine. Marx felt socially inferior and professionally jealous. He told Engels that Lassalle's "Workers' Programme" was "a bad vulgarization of the *Manifesto* and of other ideas which we have expounded so often that they have become more or less commonplaces," and in letter after letter he poured out personal abuse of Lassalle: "This combination of Jewry and Germany with a fundamental Negro streak. . . . The fellow's self-assertiveness is Negro, too." Before Lassalle left London

Marx had to borrow money from him, and he let this indebtedness foul all his subsequent relations with Lassalle.

So it came about that the first real socialist party was founded in Germany, not by Marx but in spite of Marx. He told Lassalle in London that this was no time for founding a working-class party, and he opposed all the plans which Lassalle unfolded to him for agitation among the German workers. Marx seemed to think that there must be a bourgeois revolution before there could be a proletarian movement in Germany, and he regarded Bismarck as a mere pawn of the Emperor of France, who in turn was a pawn of the Czar of Russia; but whether it was this misunderstanding of the German situation or merely his personal jealousy of Lassalle that led him to oppose the formation of a German party is uncertain.

Back in Germany, Lassalle plunged into agitation with a verve that has rarely been surpassed in revolutionary history. In January 1863 when he was put on trial in Berlin for his "Workers' Programme," he turned the court into a sounding-board for socialist propaganda. Two months later he was telling Germany that : "A party of labour now exists. This party must be provided with a theoretical understanding and with a practical war-cry even if it cost me my head three and thirty times." By May the party was organized as the General Union of German Workers.

If proof be needed of the success of Lassalle's agitation, it is to be found in Bismarck's reaction to it. The Minister-President invited Lassalle to come and see him. Together they discussed the question of the working-class. From Bismarck's point of view its organization would be a useful counterforce to middle-class liberalism. They could agree on their dislike of bourgeois liberals, and they had something in common, too, in their view of the State, which Lassalle saw not in the Marxist light of an instrument of class domination but as "a unity of individuals in a moral whole." While Bismarck played with the idea of using Lassalle's party against the liberals, Lassalle urged Bismarck to introduce universal suffrage, and to set up a Parliament in which workers' representatives might vote for State loans for workers' productive associations. He took a high tone with the Minister-President when he sent him a copy of the rules of the General Union; his covering letter said : "Herewith I send your Excellency the Constitution of my realm, for which you will perhaps envy me."

The interviews came to nothing, and soon Lassalle was stumping the country again and Bismarck's officials were following him with bans on political discussion and on tendentious newspapers. Bismarck judged his repressive measures nicely. In October 1863 when the Liberal Party won a success in the elections, Lassalle's lecture tours were allowed to succeed, but when 1864 came and Bismarck had the stage set for the Prussian war against Denmark, he no longer needed his help against liberals; the new provinces—Schleswig-Holstein and Lauenburg—would be enough to keep the bourgeoisie quiet. Meanwhile Lassalle worked his campaign to a crashing crescendo and himself to the verge of a breakdown. The crescendo reached its climax at the end of June when a huge crowd of workers gathered at Düsseldorf station to see Lassalle off. The breakdown followed two months later. Lassalle was in love with a girl called Helen von Dönniges, madly enough in

love to challenge her father and her fiancé, a Ru-
manian nobleman, von Rakowitz, to a duel. Von
Rakowitz accepted the challenge and chose to fight
with pistols. Lassalle was shot in the abdomen and
died of the wound.

It was an unworthy death from the point of view
of socialist history, but it left Lassalle none the less a
martyr in the eyes of the German working-class. He
had done something which Marx would have given
his eyes to do : he had founded the first strong socialist party in the world, a party which, though it had
only 4,610 members when Lassalle died, would
prove indestructible. He had proved that the working-class awakening of the early 1860s could be
organized in the communist cause. Marx was jealous
and said some terrible things of Lassalle in later
years, but a note of sincerity was struck in a line
written to Countess Hatzfeldt in 1864 : "Even aside
from his abilities, I personally loved him. The un-
fortunate thing is that we concealed it from one another as if we were going to live for ever."

Meanwhile the socialist awakening had spread to
France. People were taking some notice of Proudhon now. He was beginning to have a following, not
only among intellectuals but among working people.
There was a public that not only read him but
thought of acting on his advice. In April 1863 he
published a pamphlet on universal suffrage (*Les
Démocrates assermentés*), in which he urged democrats to abstain from voting at the May elections.
The number of abstentions was a record : it was esti-
mated that Proudhon had 40,000 followers on this
issue. In the following year there was a more tangible
sign of his influence. A group of Paris working-men,

led by a bronze-worker called Tolain, had made up their minds, against the advice of the middle-class leaders of the Left parties, to put forward proletarians as candidates for the next elections. They published the famous Sixty-man Manifesto (*Manifeste des Soixante*) and consulted Proudhon about it. Proudhon was delighted: "The Social Revolution is advancing much quicker than may seem," he said.

Now, when at last the working-class was recognizing Proudhon as a leader, it was too late. Proudhon, who had been battling for his life against the suffocation of asthma ever since his return to Paris, was near the end of his strength. He could neither walk nor lie down; sleeping and eating were as difficult as climbing a mountain. "I am atrociously ill," he wrote in January 1863, "my head feels like a barrel, and I've got to the stage of enervation when I can't digest and when to take a few paces makes me sea-sick." In this state he forced himself to undertake another year's work, finishing the Federation book and the pamphlet on suffrage, roughing out a sixty-page pamphlet on the Treaties of 1815 and a book on the Principles of Art dedicated to his friend Gustave Courbet. He looked forward to taking a summer holiday in the Franche-Comté, but when August came he could not afford the fare and had to content himself with a few excursions to the Bois de Boulogne and Meudon. He was seriously worried now by failing health and lack of money. Garnier's were offering handsome advances if he would only write on literature instead of sociology, and half a dozen Paris papers were soliciting literary contributions. But Proudhon had still something to say on the science of society, and his journalistic ambition was still to have a paper of his own (in 1863 he was refused permission to launch a weekly with the title *Fédération*). Apart from ill-health and worry, he felt himself to be at the top of his form.

A letter to Burzen, written in November 1863, contains a pleasant character sketch of himself—"a man who has made writing his job, who has produced a few more or less satisfactory pages, a man who, impassioned by the ideas of justice and liberty to the point of setting himself against the tide of events and of opinion, attacking men and things, celebrities and superstitions, etc.; and at the same time a good fat peasant, simple to the point of banality, well-meaning to the point of silliness, rustic, often coarse, full of inconsiderateness, common, vulgar, sometimes inert and indifferent, sometimes carried away and unbalanced, extremely curt and the very opposite of distinguished, urbane or polished; a man who finds himself only in the excitement of war and in the heat of controversy." How little he admired this character can be seen in a letter, written a month later: "To be a man, to raise oneself above the things that happen to us here below, to fashion ourselves in the divine image, as the Bible says, to realize on earth the reign of the spirit—that is the object of life. But this is not to be attained in youth or even in manhood, certainly not by great works of production or in business struggles; it is to be attained in complete maturity, when the passions begin to die down and the soul, more and more liberated, spread its wings towards the infinite."

In 1864 the most serious illness of his life overtook Proudhon. After five months of intense catarrh and asthma, he had an attack of erysipelas complicated by abscesses on the neck, which kept him in bed, unable to read or collect his thoughts, for thirty-seven days. By July the doctors pronounced him out of danger, but it would be a full month before he would be fit for work. Over half a year lost and not a penny earned! He wrote to Delhasse asking for two thousand francs. His liabilities were increasing, but there were good assets on his desk in the form of manuscripts and rough drafts of half a dozen books. All that he had to do was to get well. He would take a few weeks in the Franche-Comté, as he had promised to do in the previous summer, and come back a lion refreshed. Towards the end of August he set out in the careful company of an old friend, Dr. Cretin, who had come to him as a young disciple in 1848. He went to Dampierre to stay with an even older doctor friend, Maguet, one of the little group of students round Fallot and Ackermann in the first Paris days. From Dampierre he went to Besançon, where he had few relatives left and only one patron. In the library where he had made his first studies as a barefooted boy, the same librarian who had given him his first encouragement was still at the desk. M. Weiss was now eighty-six. Proudhon had always admired him: "It is my opinion," he had written to Maurice in 1860, "that M. Weiss is, in his genre, one of the most learned, worthy and witty men in France, one of the last and most honourable representatives of the eighteenth century, which, in individual human beings, was worth more than the nineteenth." The old gentleman received Proudhon as a son and a celebrity, asking to be given a photograph and a signed copy of the *Majorats Littéraires*. It was the most touching compliment that Proudhon had ever been paid.

Proudhon knew that he was rounding off his life. Back in Paris he pretended that he had found a way of living without health—"You will see that instead of getting better I shall end by getting used to being ill," he wrote to Beslay in October—but when the full damp of autumn began to settle on his lungs, he had little hope of living through the winter. Happily there were for once no money worries; Garnier had offered him an advance of 10,000 francs a year. Happily there was someone to help him in his endless work; after November, when he could no longer hold a pen, his letters were dictated to his daughter, who signed them : "Pour mon père, Cathérine Proudhon." There was little else to be happy about. His work would have to be unfinished : the book on woman (*La Pornocratie, ou les femmes dans les temps modernes*), the book on the origins of Christianity (*Césarisme et Christianisme*), the work on France and the Rhine, and others, all left in unrevised manuscript; and two little books in proof still to be corrected—*Nouvelles observations sur l'unité italienne* and *De la Capacité des classes ouvrières*. The last word printed during his life would re-echo the first : "Born and bred in the bosom of the working-class, belonging to it still in common suffering and aspirations, my greatest joy would surely be to be enabled henceforth to work without cease, through science and philosophy, with all the energy of my will and all the forces of my spirit, for the betterment, moral and intellectual, of those whom I delight to call my brothers and my companions."

On 19 January 1865 Proudhon died. The next day when a great crowd, including thousands of working people, gathered to follow the coffin to the cemetery, the Grande Rue of Passy awoke to realize that it had housed a famous man.

## Chapter Nine

# The Proudhonist Tradition

LASSALLE'S ambition had been confined to forming a German working-class party; Marx's intention was to found an international organization. This had been his aim ever since he had invited Proudhon to join his correspondence society in 1844, and it was expressed in the slogan with which he concluded the Communist Manifesto of 1848: "Workers of all countries, unite!" Nothing could be done about it in the doldrums which followed the failure of the 1848 revolutions, but the awakening of the 1860s offered an opportunity.

Napoleon III, anxious to propitiate the working-class in France, had allowed 200 representatives elected by their fellow-workers to go to London for the Great Exhibition in 1861. A group of English trade unionists organized a "fraternal celebration" to greet them. In the following year a further meet-took place in London to make propaganda for the now popular cause of Polish independence. When the English workers' committee, headed by Odger the shoemaker and Beesley the Professor of History in London University, sent their letter of thanks to the Paris workers for their support, a new note was sounded. The letter referred to the pressure which English employers were able to exert on workers agitating for higher wages by importing cheap foreign labour. If workers in the various countries had closer contact, this would not happen. The Frenchmen responded quickly to this appeal and sent a delegation to London. A mass meeting was called in St. Martin's Hall, on 28 September 1864, to discuss international action in strikes; there were delegates from Germany, Italy and Switzerland, as well as from France and Britain. It was at this meeting that the International Working Men's Association was founded.

Marx was in no sense responsible for all this, and although he attended the meeting as a German representative, the point of view of the German workers was voiced not by him but by Eccarius. When a General Council of fifty-five delegates and a drafting committee to draw up the rules of the association were set up, Marx found himself a member of both.

The problem for Marx now was how to get into a position from which he could dominate and direct the International Working Men's Association. It would not be easy; it would call for tact and self-effacement, qualities which Marx had never shown before and never showed again, but which he exercised remarkably in the years between 1864 and 1869. Perhaps this was due to changes in his personal life, in which the year 1863 was to some extent a turning-point. In 1863 he was still penniless, still filling his letters to Engels with requests for more money, which Engels was in no position to send. In that year occurred his one and only quarrel with his benefactor. Engels's mistress, Mary Burns, died, and Engels was heartbroken. Marx wrote a letter saying that Mary had been "good-natured, witty and devoted," and going on to bemoan at great length his own financial plight. Engels was shocked and hurt.

He replied: "Dear Marx, you will understand that this misfortune of mine and your frigid attitude towards it have made it impossible for me to reply to you before. . . ." Marx apologized and the rift was healed, but the incident demonstrated the uncertain control that Marx had over himself in 1863. By the next year he was a different man. A German colleague died and left him £800. At the same time Engels was made a partner in his father's firm and could send Marx all the money he needed. He could work now with an easy mind, getting the drafts of the second and third volumes of his *magnum opus* on to paper and seeing the first through the press; that first volume of *Capital* was published by Meissner of Hamburg in September 1867.

Whatever the reason may be, Marx in his later forties was at his best. The Rules and Inaugural Address which he drew up for the International were a model of statesmanship. They were drafted to reconcile the various factions in the association. The largest faction was the English, who were trade unionists caring nothing about the historic destiny of the proletariat, of which they had never heard, but working like beavers for universal suffrage and for the organization of strikes to raise their standard of living. The second largest was the French, who were Proudhonists to a man, full of ideas about mutual credit and co-operation and wanting no political action at all. Then there were the Italians, followers of Mazzini and thinking of nothing but their own nationalist cause, and the Germans, headed by Schweitzer, the disciple of Lassalle, who were distrustful of the whole idea of the International.

Marx established control over the International without anybody's knowing that he was doing so.

As Nikolaievsky said: "Socialists in France were either Proudhonists or Blanquists, with here and there an isolated Saint-Simonian. But there were no French Marxists. Not one in a hundred members of the International in France knew that the leader of the Central Council in London was a German named Karl Marx. In the other Latin countries the situation was the same. . . . In England Marx was less known than anywhere else."

Marx directed operations from behind the scenes. He did not attend the plenary meetings of the International, either the private conference held in London in 1865, or the Geneva Congress in 1866, or the Lausanne Congress in 1867, or the Brussels Congress in 1868, or the Basle Congress in 1869. By skilful manœuvring he managed to establish himself in some degree of control of the heterogeneous association. The British trade unionists were won over by his appeal to their practical ability and common sense. The French and Belgian representatives he attempted to split. The Belgians had been nearer to Proudhon than to Marx, but several of them, notably César de Paepe, were beginning to see that only collectivism and State intervention could cope with the problems of large-scale and monopolist industries. The French representatives in London were all Proudhonists, but Marx made use of the Blanquists in France—advocates of violent revolutionary action—and succeeded in getting four of them nominated to the Geneva Congress in 1866. They were expelled, and Geneva was a triumph for the Proudhonists. The only point they lost was when Tolain proposed that professional intellectuals—such as Marx—be excluded from the Association of Workers.

What Marx felt about the Proudhonists who came

to the Geneva Congress was expressed in a letter to Kugelmann in October 1866: "These gentlemen from Paris had their heads stuffed with the most futile Proudhonist phrases. . . . Proudhon has done an enormous amount of mischief. His pseudo-criticism and his pseudo-opposition to the Utopists (he himself was merely a bourgeois Utopist, whereas in the Utopias of a Fourier or an Owen we may discern intimations and imaginative foreshadowings of a new world) first fascinated the clever young students and then the workers, especially those of Paris, who, being engaged in the production of articles of luxury, are strongly though unwittingly interested in the maintenance of the old order. Ignorant, vain, portentous, talkative—mere windbags—they were on the verge of spoiling the whole affair, for their numbers at the Congress were quite disproportionate to the membership of the French section."

Triumphant at Geneva, the Proudhonists suffered a set-back at Lausanne in the following year. They were opposed to political action, but the statutes laid down firmly that such action was the means to the end of workers' emancipation. The upholders of State action won the day, and all that the Proudhonists could do was to throw out a motion for the nationalization of the land.

Marx was highly pleased with his work. "We, that is you and I," he wrote to Engels in September 1867, "have this powerful engine in our hands. *Compare this with the results of the Mazzinis', etc., operations over thirty years!* And without any financial resources! With the intrigues of the Proudhonists in Paris, of Mazzini in Italy, with the jealous Odger, Cremer and Potter in London, with Schulze-

Delitzsch and the Lassallians in Germany! We may consider ourselves very well satisfied."

Two years later Marx and Engels were anything but satisfied. Behind all the cross-currents in the working-class movements represented in the International were two major tendencies in conflict. One was the collectivism of which Marx was the architect and exponent, the other was the mutualism and anarchism associated with Proudhon. During his lifetime Proudhon's influence had been confined to France, with some repercussions in the French-speaking parts of Belgium and Switzerland, but around the time of his death in 1865 it spread to German Switzerland, Italy and Spain. Its extension was due largely to Bakunin, a prophet who had taken on the mantle of Proudhon.

Mikail Bakunin, a son of Russian country gentry, was what might be called a natural revolutionary, a natural leader of conspiracy and insurrection. His tragedy was that there was no cause for him to lead in his native Russia, which during his youth was held in the clamp of Nicholas I's tyranny; he had to spend his life in foreign fields fighting for foreign causes. When the French revolution broke out in February 1848 he rushed to Paris, where the Prefect of Police summed him up memorably: "What a man! The first day of the revolution he is a perfect treasure; but on the second day he ought to be shot." When revolution spread to Germany he rushed to Berlin, where he saw a chance of stirring the Polish colony to revolt. The vision of a pan-Slav revolution was strong in his mind, and he got to Prague in time to play a part in the Czech insurrection. With the police on his tracks he made his way to Saxony in time to urge the liberals of Dresden to fortify the city against the Prussian troops who were being sent to restore order. In the end he was caught. He was imprisoned in Dresden, condemned to death and led out to execution, but the sentence was commuted to life imprisonment. Then he was handed over to the Austrians, and imprisoned in Prague, his sentence commuted. The Austrians passed him on to the Russians, who imprisoned him in the Peter-Paul Fortress, and tortured him to the point of extracting a typically Russian confession. After prison treatment which would have killed any other man, his sentence was changed to exile for life in Siberia, whence after four years he succeeded in making his escape—by way of Japan and America—to Europe.

He arrived in 1863 brimming over with the ideas which had dominated Europe thirteen years ago. He would devote himself to the destruction of the Austrian Empire and to the creation of a free federation of the Slav peoples. He would begin with the Poles, who were in insurrection again. His intervention came to nothing : he got as far as mid-Baltic with a collection of Poles in a chartered English ship, but the captain turned the ship about and took them back to Denmark. Bakunin then settled—if such a word may be used of him—in Switzerland, where he devoted himself to the liberation not only of the oppressed nationalists but to that of the workers of the world.

He was a giant of a man, passionate, generous, unco-ordinated and not a little mad, though there was a shrewdness in him and occasionally some clearness of sight. No one saw more clearly into the characters of Marx and Proudhon and into the issues which would divide their disciples. "Marx," he wrote, "is a serious and profound economic thinker, and he has the tremendous advantage over Proudhon of being a materialist. Despite all his efforts to free himself from the traditions of classical idealism, Proudhon remained an incorrigible idealist all his life, swayed at one moment by the Bible and at the next by Roman Law (as I told him two minutes before he died) and always a metaphysician to his finger-tips. His great misfortune was that he never studied natural science and never adopted its methods. He possessed sound instincts, and they fleetingly showed him the correct path; but misled by bad or idealist habits of his intellect he fell back again and again into his old errors. Then Proudhon became a permanent contradiction, a powerful genius and a revolutionary thinker who fought ceaselessly against the illusions of realism but never succeeded in defeating them for good. . . . As a thinker Marx is on the right path. He has set up the principle that all religious, political and legal developments in history are not the cause but the effect of economic developments. This is a great and fruitful idea, but not all the credit for it is due to him. Many others before him had a hand in the unveiling of it and even expressed it in part, but in the last resort credit is due to him for having developed the idea scientifically and having made it the basis of his whole scientific teaching. On the other hand, Proudhon understood the idea of freedom better than Marx. When not engaged in inventing doctrines and fantasies, Proudhon possessed the authentic instinct of the revolutionary; he respected Satan and proclaimed anarchy. It is quite possible that Marx will develop an even more reasonable idea of freedom than did Proudhon, but he lacks Proudhon's instinct. As a German and a Jew he is an authoritarian from head to heels."

Bakunin, like Proudhon, had "an instinct for freedom," but he had no capacity at all for working out
any "reasonable idea" of it, and very little for organizing the working-class movement in a way that
would save it from Marx's authoritarianism and yet
leave it still an organization. He joined the radical
League for Peace and Freedom in Geneva and tried
to get the Workers' International to accept an alliance with it. When Marx made the International
refuse this alliance, he formed a splinter-group of the
League into an International Alliance for Social
Democracy. This Alliance, which had members in
Italy and Spain as well as in France and in Switzerland, regarded itself as a branch of the International.
Marx hated it, calling its programme "an *olla
podrida* of worn-out platitudes, an empty rigmarole,
a rosary of pretentious notions to make the flesh
creep, a banal improvisation aiming at not having
more than a temporary effect." He saw Bakunin as
a danger, not only because his attempts at organizing
seemed likely to bring the followers of Proudhon together into a movement, but because Bakunin had
what Marx and Proudhon both lacked, an inspiring
public presence and a gift for galvanizing a mass
meeting.

The Basle Congress of the International, which
was held in September 1869, was a duel between
Marx and Proudhon. Neither was present : Proudhon was dead and Marx stayed in London. But
Marx from his position on the General Council had
organized the agenda and set the policy of the platform, and had a spokesman in Eccarius, the German
tailor, while the disciples of Proudhon were led by
Bakunin very much in person. The central motion
on which the seventy-eight delegates had to vote

(they claimed to represent workers in England, France, Belgium, Switzerland, Austria, Italy, Spain and the United States) was a motion for the abolition of the right of inheritance. This was proposed by Bakunin and opposed by the Marxist Central Council on the ground that the right of inheritance was but a symptom of private property and that what should be abolished was the disease itself. Neither Bakunin nor the Marxists got a clear majority, but the significant fact was that the Central Council failed, for the first time in a Congress of the International, to get its way on a major issue.

It was decided at Basle that the next Congress should be held in Paris in September 1870, but on 19 July the Franco-Prussian War broke out. Marx's reaction to this was typical. In a letter to Engels in July he wrote: "The French need a thrashing," etc. The reaction of Bakunin was equally typical. "France must be saved by anarchy," he wrote in an open letter in September 1870 when the French army had been defeated at Sedan. "The necessity is that every commune should rise and then force the German army to capitulate." In the same month he attempted in Lyons a *coup de main* which was to be the beginning of a revolutionary rising. It was a pitiful failure, but Bakunin's ideas inspired the Marseilles rising which was to follow, and the Paris Commune itself.

The Commune owed nothing to the Workers' International; Engels admitted in 1871 that "the International did not raise a finger to make the Commune." It began as an insurrection of Parisians against the Government of the French National Assembly which had decided to remove from Montmartre the guns which had been placed there to keep them out of the hands of the Prussians. The insurrectionists formed a Commune of seventy-eight members, most of whom were Blanquists though several of the leaders, notably Beslay, were Proudhonists, and such ideology as the movement possessed was Proudhon's idea of a federation of communes. The Paris Commune was drowned in a blood-bath after a week of street fighting and massacres in May 1871. Its importance in socialist history is the myth of the International which arose from it. Marx presented an address to the International's General Council on *The Civil War in France*, in which he praised the Commune and urged the International to take over its heritage. This was enough to convince European Governments that the International was a powerful underground movement, full of menace for them all; none of them would allow it to hold an open Congress again. An ill-attended conference met in London in 1871 with Marx in the chair; it did little but attack Bakunin and his followers for having formed a federal organization in the Jura. Another minor conference met at The Hague in 1872, and here Marx's attempts at centralized control led to a general breakaway. The English, terrified by the violence of the Commune, formed no autonomous federation. The Blanquists, led by Vaillant, resigned. Bakunin was excluded and his followers walked out. Marx thereupon worked for a vote to shift the headquarters of the association from London to New York. Thus he hoped to bury the International which he had done so much to found but had been unable to control.

Such international organization as survived Marx's *coup de grâce* was in the Proudhonist tradition as interpreted—and transmogrified—by Bakunin. There were Bakuninist bodies, calling themselves federations within the International, in the Jura, in Italy (especially in Bologna), in Spain where the republican movement of 1873 was to some extent stimulated by them, and among the Walloons of Belgium. Congresses of a sort were held almost annually until 1877, and even after that the idea of an Anarchist International was not dead.

The influence of Proudhon had been strong in Bakunin's brand of revolutionary anarchism, but the nihilistic anarchism of the assassins who gave the police of Europe so much trouble in the last quarter of the century had no more to do with Proudhon than it had with Marx. Proudhon's ideas had spread to Russia through his friend Herzen and his acquaintance Tolstoi, but the Russian who did most to develop his ideas on the side of theoretical anarchism was Prince Kropotkin (1842–1921), whose journal, *La Révolte*, published in Switzerland, and whose pamphlets and books written in French and English and translated into many languages, had a great influence on Left-wing thought if not on political organization and action. Kropotkin was instrumental in organizing an International Workers' Alliance in 1881, making some sort of an association between anarchists in France, Italy, Spain and the United States.

Anarchism was now developing on three distinct planes. There was the philosophic anarchism of which Kropotkin was the leading exponent, which tried—and failed—to find a way of extending the "natural" social units to some all-embracing society that would still be free from coercion. There was the practical anarchism of the small community which had been so dear to Proudhon, the co-operative group of producers and consumers. Finally, there was the anarcho-syndicalism of the factory workers who put their faith in the producer groups (trade unions or *syndicats*), foreseeing a time when these would take over the factories and the raw materials and, by interlocking syndicalist federations, come to organize the economic life of the modern industrial nation. All those types of anarchism were well represented in the United States by immigrants from various parts of Europe. There was even a "pure" Proudhonist sect in Boston under W. A. Greene.

The Proudhonist tradition came to Spain in 1868. In that year Pi y Margall translated Proudhon's *Du Principe Fédératif* into Spanish. Pi was a Catalan whose anarchism became more moderate after the failure of the 1854 revolution, and who had become leader of the new Federal movement which aimed at replacing the centralized government by a voluntary federation of autonomous cantons, these cantons being themselves divided into free municipalities. Proudhon's book provided the theory which the movement had hitherto lacked. When King Amadeo resigned and the Republic was proclaimed in June 1873, Pi y Margall was elected president. His federal experiment broke down after a couple of months, but the ideal has lived on in Spain to this day.

The year 1868 also saw the establishment of a Bakuninist organization in Spain. Bakunin sent Fanelli, an Italian engineer, to Barcelona to found a Spanish branch of the International. In this Fanelli did not succeed, but a Spanish Alliance of Social Democracy was formed in 1870 with a Bakuninist programme, "in politics anarchist, in economy collectivist, in religion atheist." After bitter disputes between Marxists and Bakuninists the Spanish International was finally founded as an anarchist, decentralized organization in 1873. Its members took little part in the Republic of that year, of which the middle-class Federals bore the heat and burden, but anarchism survived to become the main working-class movement in Spain.

Spanish anarchism was strongest in Catalonia and Andalusia. In the latter it was essentially a rural movement; the small southern hill-town or village was still a more or less self-sufficient community, owning its own fields and grazing lands and having its own traditions, and resenting the intrusion of external government of any kind. In the towns of Catalonia anarchism developed a different character. The problem there was how to apply anarchist principles to an urban society. The answer was found in the trade unions. Spanish anarcho-syndicalism was influenced by Proudhon's puritanism and by Sorel's *mystique* of the General Strike, but the Spanish trade unions were unlike any that could be found in France; they had no schemes for social insurance, no strike pay, often no subscriptions, and their secretaries and administrators were not paid. In 1910 anarchist unions formed the Confederación Nacional del Trabajo (C.N.T.), in opposition to the socialist-union organization, the U.G.T. The C.N.T. was strong enough in its anarchism to brave the communist winds which blew from Moscow after 1917 but, rather than face suppression by the dictator Primo de Rivera, it dissolved itself in 1923. A few years later a secret society, the Federación Anarquista Iberica (F.A.I.) was founded to inspire and control the C.N.T. as soon as it should be allowed to re-establish itself, which happened in 1930 after the fall of Primo de Rivera. The C.N.T. became the only really revolutionary trade-union movement in

the world. It could be argued that Spanish anarchism was in a purely Spanish tradition and owed
nothing to the outside world, but Catalonia, where
anarchism was strongest, has always been in close
touch with France, and the writings of Proudhon,
Bakunin and Sorel were read and followed there to
an extent which would have surprised their authors.

The influence of Proudhon's ideas was naturally
most direct and enduring in France. Many young republicans in the last years of the Second Empire—
for instance, Gambetta, an impassioned reader of
*De la Justice*—were Proudhonists, at least in their
fear of an intransigent Jacobin centralization of
power. There was a continued pressure for a Proudhonist organization of credit, sustained by Damiron
in *La Presse* and by Georges Duchêne in closely argued books against the evils of high finance. In the
socialist camp, the two sons-in-law of Karl Marx,
Langlois and Longuet, were Proudhonists before
they were Marxists, and so was Jules Guesde, later
to become the leading Marxist in French party politics. In fact there was no Marxist socialist movement
in France before 1877, and for a decade or more
after that it made only slow progress. All French
working-class organizations were Proudhonist in
1865, and when trade unions were at last fully legalized in 1884 it was by Proudhonist workers that the
new, large, peaceable industrial syndicates as well as
the small, revolutionary craft unions were built up.
A *Fédération Nationale des Syndicats* formed in
1886 became a battle-ground between Marxists and
Proudhonists, and when the former looked like getting control of it, a new syndicalist movement sprang
up round the federation of local unions known as the
Bourses du Travail. The struggle between Marxist

and Proudhonist traditions went on, especially on the question of the constitution of the Confédération Générale du Travail, which was first established in 1895 and altered again and again.

By the first years of the twentieth century Proudhonism had prevailed in the French trade-union movement. It had abandoned some of the master's ideas on tactics, rejecting, for example, his anti-strike views. It had been inspired by new teachers, particularly Georges Sorel whose *Avenir Socialiste des Syndicats* (1897) reaffirmed the anti-State, non-political principles of Proudhon. The victory of the Proudhon tradition came at the Amiens Congress of the C.G.T. in 1906, when a charter was adopted separating the trade unions from the political movement. "In order that syndicalism may exercise its maximum effect, industrial action should be brought to bear directly against the employers; the organizations belonging to the Confederation have no business, *qua* trade-union groups, to preoccupy themselves with parties or sects, which, outside and alongside the syndicalist movement, can pursue the transformation of society in their own way." It would be a long time before French trade unionists were to abandon the idea that to send members to Parliament was useless, because, once they had become members they would no longer be workers or trade unionists or even capable of expressing the feelings of the socialist masses; socialist workers should leave politics and religion alone and concentrate on the factory; once they were in charge of the factory, the syndicates would form the basis of the new society.

Yet it is misleading to attempt to trace the influence of Proudhon in institutional terms. Before the First World War, French socialism had become officially Marxist on its political side, though as late as 1936 Professor Elie Halévy was telling his pupils at the Ecole des Sciences Politiques that "the real inspirer of French socialism is not Marx but the individualist Proudhon." Before the Second World War, French trade unionism had turned to politics and was becoming the prey of parties and sects, but if one asks oneself in what respect trade unionism in France differs from trade unionism in other West European countries, the answer must be in the influence of Proudhon's ideas.

## Chapter Ten

# The Marxist Tradition

AFTER his failure with the International in 1872, Marx was never the same man again. His hopes and those of his colleagues for immediate revolution, so lively in the 1860s, had been dashed by Bismarck's victory. His attempt to organize the working-class internationally had broken down. He was suffering, too, from a breakdown in his health. His appearance was still striking. Lafargue, his son-in-law, saw "a man above middle height, with broad shoulders and a deep chest, his limbs well proportioned on the whole, though his legs were rather too short for his body (as is apt to be the case in members of the Jewish race)," and Hyndman, the English politician, noted that "he combined in his own person and nature, with his commanding forehead and great overhanging brow, his fierce glittering eyes, broad, sensitive nose and mobile mouth, all surrounded by a setting of untrimmed hair and beard, the righteous fury of the great seers of his race with the cold analytical power of Spinoza and the Jewish doctors." Yet he was a sick man, ravaged with a liver disease and diabolically tortured by insomnia, and he could not regain his old capacity for work. There were the second and third volumes of *Capital* to be written, but he never got beyond the drafting of the second volume and the desultory collection of more material, most of it on Russia; in the last ten years of his life he published nothing beyond a few articles.

These were sad years, too, for the whole working-class movement. In France the repression which followed the Commune obliterated socialist and trade-union organizations for more than a decade. Trade unions in all countries were driven on to the defensive by the economic recession of the middle seventies. Prices were falling, and agricultural depression was followed by industrial recession and unemployment. Only in Germany in its first surge of industrial development were circumstances propitious for the working-class movement.

The best of Marx's energies after 1872 went into the attempt to build up a working-class party in Germany. Here the first task, as he saw it, was to destroy the Lassallian influence. Back in 1864 he had sent his disciple Liebknecht to Saxony, where the young wood-turner Bebel already had a following among the Workmen's Educational Societies. Within a few years Bebel and Liebnecht had organized these societies into an association with 14,000 members, and had split them from the Lassallians and formed a separate party. In 1875 representatives of the two parties met at Gotha and decided to merge them in a single German Social Democratic Workers' Union, with a programme that was at least as Marxist as it was Lassallian. Marx and Engels should have been pleased with this, but they were not. They were furious with Liebknecht for not gaining control before entering into negotiations with the Lassallians, and they were bitterly opposed to the Gotha programme. Marx sent a long memorandum (known after its publication by Engels years later as the *Critique of the Gotha Programme*) which Liebknecht read and decided to suppress. It attacked the programme for being Proudhonist, and went on to a re-statement of the old questions of dispute with Lassalle; and the point of it was that the Gotha agreement made concessions to the Lassallians which were quite unnecessary because the Lassallians were on the downgrade and would have accepted fusion on much less favourable terms.

In fact, the fusion was wholly to the advantage of the Marxists. It brought the Lassallian masses into the party while leaving control to Liebknecht, Bebel and their colleagues. Bismarck's government was turning against the socialist movement in all its forms, and the Lassallian policy of alliance with the State against the middle-classes was thereby discredited. The party went from strength to strength. It won 493,000 votes at the elections of 1877, thanks largely to a financial crisis which had given scope for socialist propaganda. (Ten years later the socialist vote reached 550,000, and in 1890 it was 1,427,000.)

After the Gotha row, Marx was an invalid. He and his wife moved to the comfort of 41, Maitland Park Terrace in 1875, but there was little peace. More and more frequent visits had to be made to spas—first in Germany, then in France and England —to take the waters for what had now been definitely diagnosed as an enlarged liver. His daughters had left home : the younger, Laura, had married Lafargue, a Cuban of mixed blood. Jenny had married Longuet who, after his part in the Commune, had become a lecturer in London. Soon they moved to Paris, whence the speeches and writings of neither son-in-law came as much consolation to Marx. "Longuet as the last Proudhonist, and Lafargue as the last Bakuninist ! The Devil take them !" Fortunately there were grandchildren to cheer Marx's declining years and visitors to flatter his vanity. In 1880 Bebel came from Germany to confer with Marx and Engels. Guesde came from France to get their advice in the formation of the new French socialist federation. There was even an English disciple, the Etonian Hyndman who had read *Capital* and had been inspired by it. In 1881 Hyndman published a Marxist booklet, *England for All*, in the preface to which he acknowledged his debt "to the work of a great thinker and original writer, which will, I trust, shortly be made accessible to the majority of my countrymen." But Marx could not forgive Hyndman, the founder of the English Social Democratic Federation, for not having praised him by name.

In that same year came a blow to something deeper than vanity. Jenny Marx died of cancer in December. It was surprising to Marx that he could live without her. He had pleurisy now, but it did not kill him. Then, thirteen months later, his eldest daughter, Jenny Longuet, died suddenly. From this last blow Marx did not recover. He lingered on until he was nearly sixty-five, dying at last on 14 March 1883.

Engels made the funeral speech at Highgate Cemetery. "As Darwin discovered the law of evolution in organic matters, so Marx discovered the law of evolution in human history—the single fact, previously hidden in ideological growths, that human beings must first of all eat, drink, shelter and clothe themselves before they can turn their attention to politics, science, art and religion; that therefore the production of the immediate means of life and consequently the given stage of economic development of a people or of a period forms the basis on which the

State institutions, the legal principles, the art and even the religious ideas of the people in question have developed and out of which they must be explained, instead of exactly the contrary, as was previously attempted. But not only this. Marx discovered the special law of development of the present-day capitalist mode of production and of the bourgeois system of society which it has produced. With the discovery of surplus-value, light was suddenly shed on the darkness in which all other economists, both bourgeois and socialist, had been groping."

Engels's judgement was not unrealistic as funeral orations go. It would be over-pernickety to note that the theory of surplus-value (the theory according to which the labourer's value is determined by the minimum amount necessary to keep him alive and working, yet the employer compels him to work for longer hours than are needed to make this minimum and appropriates the surplus-value for himself) had been adumbrated by earlier writers, particularly by Proudhon, who in his first essay on Property had written : "The labourer produces 10. Very well, thinks the landowner, for me he will produce 12. . . . What the landowner does, the industrialist tries in his turn. . . . To satisfy Property, the first necessity is that the worker shall produce in excess of his needs."

What was to survive of Marx's life-work was a myth based—in so far as a myth can be based on anything as tangible as the written word—on the first volume of *Capital*. Published in German in 1867, the first translation came out—to Marx's surprise—in Russian in 1872, the French translation not appearing in complete form until 1875. No English translation was available until four years after Marx's death. It took Engels until two years after his death to get the second volume assembled and published in Hamburg, and the third volume, which had to be pieced together from notes and articles written over a period of twenty years, did not come out until 1894. These posthumous works added little to the essential teaching of Marx, which is all in the first volume of *Capital*, to which the later volumes are appendices and the *Critique of Political Economy* (1859) a sort of prologue.

The Marxist system is based on the dogma of the labour theory of value, and it is with this that *Capital* opens. It goes on to the theory of surplus value, and thence to the law of capitalist accumulation, according to which the rich get richer while the poor get poorer. Then come some fine historical chapters, based on blue books and official reports, which leave capitalists with no excuse for the appalling conditions of life of the British worker during the generation before 1866. The mixture of abstract economic theory and concrete illustration from actuality, all bound together by the materialist conception of history and a religious view of historical inevitability, made what Cromwell would have called a "fulminous compound." Dr. E. H. Carr was not exaggerating when he wrote, half a century after Marx's death, that "*Capital* has probably exercised a greater influence, in proportion to the number of people who have read it, than any other book that has ever been written."

Little of this influence was apparent when Marx died, sixteen years after the publication of *Capital*, Vol. I. If the Marxist tradition was to survive its progenitor, it must be ideologically through the work of Engels (who had another twelve years to live) and institutionally through socialist parties, above all in Germany.

When Bismarck fell and the anti-social laws were repealed, the time had come to define the aims of the German Social Democratic Party. This was done in the Erfurt Programme of 1891, which was drawn up with the advice and adopted with the approval of Engels. The programme read like a revised version of the Communist Manifesto of 1848, but if the German Social Democrats were Marxist in words, they were far from Marxist in action. Even Kautsky, the official interpreter of the Erfurt Programme, and the champion of pure Marxism against "revisionism," was full of Lassallian ideas of State Socialism. Even in the Erfurt Programme itself the call to violence was missing, and the authors seem to have had parliamentary methods in mind, at least for the immediate future. The German Social-Democratic Party, which until the First World War was far the strongest in the world in numbers and organization, spoke with the voice of Marx, but when it came to action was always timid and law-abiding in a way which must have made Marx turn in his grave.

By the time of the Erfurt Programme there were more or less Marxist parties in most of the nations of western and central Europe. In Austria, Holland and the Scandinavian countries they followed, in general, the model of the German Social Democrats. Switzerland had its cantonal problems, and the workers' party was not organized on a federal basis until 1887. Belgium was for a long time split between Marxist Flemings and Bakuninist Walloons. British and French Marxists were to have a particularly difficult row to hoe. The English Marxist Hyndman's Social Democratic Federation was established in London in 1884, but it was soon broken on the stony ground of trade-union empiricism and Fabian gradualism, and when the British Labour Party was at last founded in 1900, it was devoid of all Marxist tradition. The French Marxist, Jules Guesde, made the first attempt to reconstruct a socialist organization in France when he founded the Parti Ouvrier Français (P.O.F.) in 1879, but by 1890 the French working-class movement was divided into at least six groupings. Besides the Guesdists, there were the Possibilists with a programme of immediately possible non-revolutionary reforms, and the Blanquists, now under Edouard Vaillant, who advocated revolution without specifying their method. Apart from these three factions, in that they put no faith in political activity, were the trade unions, fully legalized since 1884, and apart altogether from parties and associations of any sort were the unorganizable, bomb-throwing anarchists.

Surprisingly it was not from Marxists but from trade unionists that the initiative came for constituting a new Workers' International. The idea was first mooted by French Syndicalists and was taken up by British trade unionists, and their contact led to a plan for an international socialist congress in 1889, the centenary of the French Revolution, when a Universal Exhibition was being held in Paris. In the event two separate congresses met in Paris simultaneously, one of Possibilists and the other largely of Marxists. The latter included socialists from twenty nations, and from it the Second International was born. Of the 400 "delegates" who attended, the majority were French, but they were hopelessly divided among themselves. The eighty-one German delegates, led by Liebknecht and Bebel, had a well-organized party behind them; inevitably the Germans had the major voice in the new organization. From this sprang most of the contradictions in the Second International.

It was Marxist in name and should be Marxist in theory. But what was Marxist theory in the 1890s, when so many of the conditions of which Karl Marx had written, had ceased to exist? The doctrine no longer fitted the facts; therefore the doctrine must be changed. But to attempt to revise the doctrine was heresy, as Bernstein found to his cost when he was condemned by the German Social Democratic Party in 1899. A doctrinal duel between the Revisionists and the Purists in Germany reminiscent of the debates in the early Church ended in the victory of the latter.

The theoretical battle and its outcome in Germany were of little interest and no consolation to socialists elsewhere. The French had at last found a basis for forming a united Socialist Party in a speech by Millerand at Saint-Mandé in 1896 : "Here, citizens, are in my opinion the three essential points that are necessary and sufficient to characterize a socialist programme : intervention by the State to nationalize private property in the different categories of the means of production and exchange as they become ripe for social appropriation; capture of the Government through universal suffrage; international understanding between the workers." Nothing very Marxist about that. When Millerand accepted Waldeck-Rousseau's invitation to join his capitalist cabinet as Minister of Commerce and Industry, the newly achieved unity of French socialists was shattered. Guesde failed to get Millerand expelled at the Bordeaux Congress in 1903, but he had his revenge by bringing the issue of participation in capitalist cabinets and the wider issue of gradual reformism before the Amsterdam Congress of the Second International in 1904.

By this time socialists in almost every country were divided between revolutionists and gradualists. In France it was Guesde against Jaurès, the architect of French Socialist unity; in England, Hyndman against Keir Hardie; in Italy, Ferri against Turati; among the exiled Russians, Lenin against Martov; in Germany, Kautsky against Bernstein. In 1903, when the German Social Democrats polled three million votes in the Reichstag elections, the party condemned participationism, revisionism, gradualism and similar heresies at their Dresden Conference. Obviously they would enforce this view on other socialist parties when it came to a resolution before the International.

Bebel and Kautsky as well as Guesde spoke at Amsterdam in support of the motion that socialists who took part in capitalist governments should be expelled from the party. Jaurès opposed it, in a speech in which he made the 444 delegates who attended the congress hear the truth about the German Social Democratic Party. He pointed out that it had no revolutionary tradition. "And just as you lack revolutionary means of action," he went on to say, "just as you lack that force which a revolutionary tradition would give you, so also, as you well know, you have no parliamentary force. Even if you got a majority in the Reichstag, you are the only country in which a socialist majority in Parliament would not mean a socialist mastery over the country. For your Parliament is but a half Parliament, without executive power, without governmental power; its

decisions are merely advisory, and the imperial
authorities may reverse them at their will. . . . We expected from you, as all mankind did, that at your
Dresden Conference, following upon your victory of
three million votes, you would define your policy.
You cried in your newspapers '*Unser das Reich,
unser die Welt*—the Empire is ours, the world is
ours !' No, the Empire is not yet yours, since you are
not even secure enough to offer hospitality to International Socialism in your own capital. . . . You mask
your practical impotence by taking refuge in extremist theories—in formulæ of the sort that your
eminent comrade Kautsky will supply you with as
long as he has breath left in his body. . . . The adop-
tion of the Dresden resolution in this international
congress will signify that International Socialism associates in all countries and in all its parts, in all its
force, with the temporary but formidable, with the
provisionary but forced inaction of German democracy."

The resolution was passed. Jaurès accepted his
defeat and did homage to Guesde. For the next ten
years Marxism in the German version remained the
official doctrine of all the continental socialist parties.
It was sound and fury, signifying nothing. Where
significance lay was in the behaviour of socialists in
the parliamentary states : they were working in an
un-Marxist way for liberal reforms in the conditions
of the working-class, and if they can be said to have
had a sincere programme it was that which Miller-
and had enunciated at Saint-Mandé. Then in 1914
the Great War brought an end to the Second International, as the Franco-Prussian War had brought
an end to the First.

This is no place to recount the chapter of accidents

—or, as Marxists would say, the steps in the inevitable march of history—by which the mantle of Marx, which had for so long been borne by the Germans, fell to the Russians under Lenin. Marx had been typically German in his fear and hatred of Russia, but towards the end of his life he began to take an interest in the possibilities of a Russian revolution. He learned the language and studied Russian problems for the later volumes of *Capital*; after his death Engels found a pile of notes and statistics on Russia measuring two cubic metres. In the last year of his life he sent Vera Zasulich a preface for her translation of the Communist Manifesto, in which he admitted that it was possible that a Russian revolution might give the signal for a workers' rising in the West. A few years later Lenin, a boy in Kazan, was reading the first volume of *Capital*. Soon he became a Marxist of the first water, attacking Bernstein's revisionism and comparing Marxist philosophy to "a solid block of steel, from which you cannot eliminate even one basic assumption without falling into the arms of a bourgeois-reactionary falsehood."

In exile in the West, Vera Zasulich, Plekhanov and Alexrod had founded in 1883 a group which marked the beginning of the Russian Social Democratic Party. When Lenin joined them it was to engineer a schism in 1903. He split the extremists under his leadership from the comparatively moderate Russian socialists under Martov, who were then advocating something resembling a popular front. Thus was born the Bolshevik Party.

The Bolshevik Revolution of 1917 put the Marxist mantle firmly on the shoulders of the Russians. Once the Revolution had indubitably succeeded and

Russia was in the Bolsheviks' hands, the Marxist tradition was theirs to make or to mar. Socialist parties outside Russia had to decide whether to be Marxist in the Russian sense—revolutionary and with strict party discipline—or socialist in the re-formist sense, playing the parliamentary-democratic game and working for piecemeal reforms. In the new phraseology, they had to decide whether to be Communist or Socialist.

For the party in Britain the decision was easy. It had never paid even lip-service to Marxism, and it was a Labour rather than an essential socialist party. But for parties in the continental countries decision was difficult and sooner or later was seen to be impossible. The German Social Democratic Party split, and socialists fought communists in open battle. The French were divided at the Tours Conference in 1922, and the communists, who found themselves in the majority, took over the party newspaper *Humanité*—and continued to publish it as "fondé par Jean Jaurès"—while the socialist minority went on calling themselves by the party's old official title, the *Section française de l'Internationale Ouvrière*. For the whole of the following generation no party conflicts in Europe were more bitter than those between the successors of the workers' parties which had come together in the Second International.

In the Russian interpretation Marxism underwent —as was right and proper—a revision every decade or so, and the ghost of Karl Marx must often have echoed a remark once made by the living Marx : "Thank God I am not a Marxist!" But the thread of the Marxist tradition, though stretched and twisted, was unbroken. The Russians were as religiously devoted to the words of the Master as ever German

Marxists had been, and they made the study of a selection of his writings compulsory for every member of secondary schools, technical colleges and universities throughout the Soviet Union. By the middle of the twentieth century Marxism was the professed creed of every state from East Germany to China, and its nominal adherents included perhaps a third of the world's population.

But the Marxist tradition, like the Christian tradition, is not only a matter of doctrine—it is a matter also of the imitation of the Master. What persisted among communists was the temper as well as the teaching of Marx. The vindictive hatred with which Karl Marx had pursued every colleague who was not an obedient disciple was copied in every communist régime. The authoritarianism and intolerance which had been characteristic of Marx himself continued to characterize the party and governmental officials who were to act in his name. It could all have been predicted, as Proudhon indeed predicted it when he wrote this definition of communism as long ago as 1864 : "A compact democracy having the appearance of being founded on the dictatorship of the masses, but in which the masses have no more power than is necessary to ensure a general serfdom in accordance with the following precepts and principles borrowed from the old-absolutism : indivisibility of public power, all-consuming centralization, systematic destruction of all individual, co-operative and regional thought [regarded as disruptive], inquisitorial police."

# A Note on Books

## MARX

A number of Marx's works have been published in English by Lawrence and Wishart. A good translation of Vol. I of *Capital* is by E. and C. Paul, in the Everyman Library; the only translation of Vols. II and III is by E. Untermann, published by Kerr in Chicago.

The standard biography is F. Mehring, translated by E. Fitzgerald (1930). A good recent study is I. Berlin, *Karl Marx, his Life and Environment* (1939), in the Home University Library. Lively expositions of his ideas will be found in G. D. H. Cole, *The Meaning of Marxism* (1948), and in A. Gray, *The Socialist Tradition* (1952). There is a good recent bibliography in H. C. Desroches and C. Hubert, *La Signification du Marxisme* (1948). A useful compilation of extracts in E. Burns, *A Handbook of Marxism* (1935).

## PROUDHON

Scarcely any of Proudhon's works are available in English translation. There is an excellent but still unfinished collection of his *Œuvres Complètes*, edited by C. Bouglé and H. Moysset (Rivière, Paris, 1920–39). Some of his *Correspondence* was published in Paris (14 vols., 1874–5), but his *Carnets* are still unpublished.

Only one biography has been written in English,

George Woodcock, *Pierre-Joseph Proudhon* (1956). The best of the French biographies is E. Dolléans, *Proudhon* (1948). Saint-Beuve's essay on Proudhon is reprinted together with Daniel Halévy's *La Jeunesse de Proudhon* in D. Halévy, *La Vie de Proudhon* (1948). See also J. Bourgeat, *Proudhon, père du socialisme français* (1942). There is a convenient selection of extracts in L. Maury, *La Pensée vivante de Proudhon* (2 vols., 1942).

## SOCIALISM

The most useful general survey is G. D. H. Cole, *History of Socialist Thought* (1953– ), of which the first three volumes describe developments down to 1914. H. W. Laidler's book of the same title was reissued as *Social-Economic Movements* in 1944. See also E. Dolléans, *Histoire du mouvement ouvrier* (3 vols., 1946–53) and, for a brief sketch, E. Halévy, *Histoire du Socialisme européen* (1948). The best books on German and French socialism are respectively F. Mehring, *Geschichte der Deutschen Sozial-Demokratie* (4 vols., revised edition, 1922) and G. Weill, *Histoire du mouvement social en France, 1852–1902* (1904).

On anarchism and syndicalism, see Max Nettlau, *Der Anarchismus von Proudhon zu Kropotkin* (1927), E. H. Carr, *Michael Bakunin* (1937), and Louis Levine, *Syndicalism in France* (1914).

On the First International there is the Anti-Marxist *L'Internationale, documents et souvenirs, 1864–1878* (4 vols., 1905–10) by James Guillaume, and the pro-Marxist *History of the First International*, by Y. M. Stekloff. On the Second, see James Joll, *The Second International* (1955).

# Index

# INDEX

Erfurt, 175
Eugénie, Empress, 113

Fallot, Gustave, 20-2, 25-6, 33, 151
Fanelli, 164
Favre, 142
Fénelon, 19
Ferri, 178
Feuerbach, 51-2, 62
Flocon, 75-6, 89
Fourier, François Marie Charles, 12, 20, 30, 32, 46, 52, 156
Franche-Comté, 27, 105, 126, 128, 148, 150
Franco-Prussian War, 161
Frankfurt Parliament, 90
Frederick William III, 39

Gambetta, 166
Gambon, 10
Garibaldi, 135, 142
Garnier (publisher), 105, 109, 114, 126, 128, 148, 151
Gassendi, 21
Gauthier, Antoine, 32
Gauthier, Frères, 18, 20, 35, 37, 70, 96
Gigot, Philippe, 60-2
Godesberg, 45
Gotha, 170-1
Gouvernet, 133
Greely, Horace, 120
Greene, W. A., 164
Greppo, 85
Grün, Karl, 57, 60, 62, 68
Guesde, Jules, 166, 172, 176-8, 180
Guizot, 58, 74

Halévy, Elie (quoted), 168
*Hallische Jahrbücher*, 43
Hardenberg, 14
Hardie, Keir, 178
Harvey, 122
Hatzfeldt, Sophie von, 143, 147
Hegel, 31, 43, 46
Heine, 51
Helvétius, 21
Herzen, 97, 112, 114, 119, 127, 163
Hess, Moses, 45-6, 51, 53
Historical Materialism, 67-8, 172-3
Holbach, 21

# INDEX

# INDEX

# INDEX

Rossi, 26
Rousseau, 31–2, 39, 141
Ruge, Arnold, 45, 48, 50, 57–8

Saint-Arnaud, 102
Saint-Mandé, 177, 179
Saint-Marc-Girardin, 26
St. Martin's Hall, 153
Saint-Simon, Claude Henri, Comte de, 12, 30, 32, 40, 46
Sainte-Pélagie, 96, 98, 104, 125
Sand, George, 125
Say, 36
Schlegel, 40
Schleswig-Holstein, 90–1
Schmeltz, 87
Schulze-Delitsch, 156–7
Schurz, 93
Schweitzer, 154
Second Republic, 75, 82, 84, 101
Siéyès, 56
Sixty-Man Manifesto, 148
Smith, Adam, 36
Soho, 118–20, 123
Sorel, Albert, 10, 165–7
Spinoza, 169
Stein, 14
Strasbourg, 26, 28, 86
Suard Prize, 21–2, 24–5, 29
Surplus Value, Theory of, 37, 173–4
Syndicalism, 9, 10, 100, 158, 160, 167

Thierry, 52
Thiers, 74, 85
*Times, The*, 93, 103
Tocqueville, Alexis de, 72–3, 77, 102–3
Tolain, 148, 155
Tolstoi, 163
Toulon, 23
Trier, 38–41, 47, 49, 58
Turati, 178

United States, 12, 161, 163–4
Urquhart, David, 121

Vaillant, Edouard, 162, 176
Vienna, 42, 90, 92
*Voix du Peuple, La*, 97–8, 114
Voltaire, 39, 113, 125, 127
*Vorwärts*, 58

# INDEX

Date